As the owner of a custom construction company, I've built projects for Ms. StJohn over the last twenty years. I know her to be both thoughtful and kind, but until I read "Holosophy," I had no idea just HOW deep and powerful her thinking really is. Wow! There are insights here to dimensions and truths I had never imagined. Better, she explains them simply and directly so they can be applied to everyday life. This incredibly readable book pulls back the curtain on how the universe really works, and a way of engaging life which is at once practical and yet far reaching. It will change your life.
~ **Tom Herman**
President, Herman Construction

The study of Holosophy has opened my mind to new areas and ways of thinking. I now have greater understanding of the level of control I have over my own life, the forces which challenge that control, and new methods to overcome them.
~ **Steve Fales**
President, AdServices

It is a rare gift to be able to speak of great ideas in the language of ordinary people. Holosophy is a gift to the world from a woman of uncommon gifts. She has given us a straight forward series of life insights, distilled into chapters and sections calculated to help people learn, grow and thrive. She passes un-noticed in the crowd, humble and un-assuming. But Jennifer is distinguished by the force of her character and the power of her presence as a friend, counselor and teacher. Find your way to Holosophy and profit by the connection.
~ **Jasmin and Paul Braslow**
Tiburon, CA

"Give a girl a fish? Or, teach a girl to fish."

A classical challenge to good intentions. How do we bring about this learning and personal growth for the greater good? Jennifer St John helped me free myself from what was holding me back. (Spoiler alert - it was me!)

I was unconsciously sabotaging myself by doing the work and carrying the burdens of others at the expense of myself.

That reality had eluded me, but through counseling, I became aware that my own blind spots were the source of my self-defeating and self-limiting thinking and behavior.

So I've "learned to fish!" So can you. Let's hear it for our guides; the "true freedom fighters" who illuminate the way.
~ **Laurie E Riegle**
Founder: Armstrong/Robitaille/Riegle
Area VP, Gallagher

Make time for this! Anything which makes life less threatening and more understandable is worth it! Holosophy is an "Investment of Time" in yourself and your ability to better meet and resolve life challenges! Read it, practice it, tell your friends and family about it and watch your world change for the better.
~ Scott Ramey
EVP Business Development
Transamerica Corporation

Success in business derives from success with people. It's about being willing to engage deeply, honestly and openly with what's actually going on. That sounds simple, and it is; if you can only shut down those "voices" in your head that tell you that "you shouldn't, you can't, you mustn't and you don't dare!" I've experienced Jennifer up close and "Holosophy" is a remarkable introduction to the secrets she's used to make winners of people in 43 countries.
~ Clara Sierra
SVP, Senior Business Development Manager
Independent Advisor Channel
Amundi Pioneer Investments

I experienced a life crisis, just about the time I received a copy of "Holosophy." What a blessing, to have the tools to separate what happened recently; from a similar challenge that occurred long ago. I might have spent years working this out; but now, I'm back on the case, with a new tool in hand. My experience has been nothing short of amazing, and I highly recommend this book for anyone motivated to make a life-changing break with old patterns and find a more free and fulfilling existence!
~ Dr. Melanie Crites-Bachert
Gresham, OR

Holosophy®

Conquering Your Fear of Success

J. R. (Jennifer) StJohn

Holosophy Foundation
1712 Pioneer Avenue, Suite 8013
Cheyenne, WY 82001
www.HolosophyFoundation.com

Copyright © 2018 by Holosophy® Foundation

All rights reserved. No part of this publication may be reproduced, distributed, or transmitted in any form or by any means, including photocopying, recording, or other electronic or mechanical methods, without the prior written permission of the publisher, except in the case of brief quotations embodied in critical reviews and certain other noncommercial uses permitted by copyright law. For permission requests, write to the publisher, addressed "Attention: Permissions Coordinator," at the address below.

Holosophy Foundation, Inc.

1712 Pioneer Avenue, Suite 8013

Cheyenne, WY 82001

Author: J. R. (Jennifer) StJohn

Photos & Illustrations: ThinkStock.com and Unsplash.com

Library of Congress Cataloging-in-Publication Data:

J.R. (Jennifer) St.John

Holosophy / by J.R. (Jennifer) StJohn

ISBN 978-0-9984445-2-9

1. Psychology 2. New Thought 3. Spirituality 4. Self-development

BF638-648 2017

155.2

Printed in the United States of America

First Edition

14 13 12 11 10 / 10 9 8 7 6 5 4 3 2 1

Acknowledgements

Book Designer: Ken West

Art Director: Tom White

Teacher and Counselor: Robert Thomas

Using this Book

Holosophy is practical philosophy; ideas that can make your life bigger, more satisfying and workable.

Read it any way you like. You're not required to proceed cover to cover! (Although, that might be a very logical, straight-ahead learning experience.)

Start with the introductory pages to get a feel for the subject. Shop the Table of Contents; absorb the flow of argument. Pick a random title you find "irritating." Turn right to that and see what you discover. Maybe you'll encounter a genuinely new idea. It may not make sense at first. Go to the dictionary and discover the alternate meanings and contexts of the words. Demand an explanation! Engage it! Wrestle with it… until a new perspective reveals itself. The biggest returns come to those who engage without reservation.

We've designed the book with larger type, images, quotes, dialogue, expository text and wider margins in which to scribble. We hope it functions as a multi-dimensional workshop: a point of entry to Holosophy.

Read, find a Counselor and begin the conversation!

Bon Voyage!

Foley's Hill

It was a beautiful summer day, and Foley's Hill beckoned. There at the the end of our street was a six block extent of steep downhill road, bottoming out in a kettle, followed by two blocks of rise, and the flat trek of a few blocks into town. It was perfect (and terrifying).

It was a rite of passage. Every kid on the block had to do it. This was my year! Came the day, and I tenuously brought my one-speed to a stop where my street met the long hill. It looked like a mile.

I pushed off. It began well! And then the pedal rotation exceeded my ability to pump, so it was legs spread wide the rest of the way, and straight into the gravel patch at the bottom…

Yeah. That wasn't a great decision. When I regained consciousness, it took a while to assess the damages. The skinned knees, elbows, shins, forehead, palms and thighs were the cardinal signs of childhood adventure. It was a long, tearful limp home, pushing the bike, then weeks of wearing the badges of failure.

The hill haunted me 'til the last week of vacation. But then, in my last heroic try, I braved it, beat it and beamed!

Still, whenever I encounter that (or any) "long hill," driving, riding or walking, I slow down a little as I break a sweat and very carefully check to make sure nothing gets out of hand. My history is with me still.

J. R. (Jennifer) StJohn

Invitation to a Dialogue

"The Truth that can be framed in words is not the Truth,
but a mere abstraction.
The finger points to the harvest moon.
Yet many see only the pointing finger."
—**Proverb**

The Debate Of Socrates And Aspasia by Nicolas-André Monsiau

The labor of love to bring Holosophy to the world has encompassed thirty-seven years. Rather than emerging fully formed, this work has evolved through a series of conversations — an ongoing dialogue — between the Founder, Robert Thomas, and the Author.

This text takes the classical form of a series of questions and answers about the nature of Holosophy, its tenets, techniques, ethical perspectives, assumptions and suppositions. It is not, in any sense, finished. As a dialogue speeds up and slows down, pauses to allow a new moment of insight to emerge, then points to a new avenue of enquiry, and ultimately reaches a point of quiescence; so this work mirrors a natural philosophical discussion. It is a *dialogue* about truth, not *the* truth.

Like all philosophical discussion, it attempts to build a model of how life functions, and a map of the interior of the mind and consciousness (no small undertaking). Yet, as with all maps, it is not the territory.

There will be points at which your perception may differ from ours. And there the fun begins!*

Bring your ideas and join the dialogue, which opens the door to a greater perception of the truth.

The Author

---

*There is no greater pleasure, or glorious pain, than being in the presence of a genius at work. Having reveled in and chafed under The Master's steady tutelage, I can tell you that real growth is never easy, but always worth it!

Contents

Using this Book viii
Foley's Hill ix
Invitation to a Dialogue xi
Book Map 1
Section 1: Preface **3**
Welcome 4
Give and Take 6
New Words 8
Colophon 10
Who Needs Holosophy? 11
Mere Survival? 14
Closer to Fine 16
Change the World 18
Summary: Enlarged Perspective 22
Section 2: Problem **25**
Problem: Overview 26
Never Again! 29
Post-Traumatic Stress 34
Sequester 37
Dirty Lens 40
Lessons Learned 45
Habitual Perception 49
Armor Against Loss 53
Redundant Reflexive Memory 55
Tendrils of Trauma 58
Mechanism of Interference 61
What We Never Question... 64
Ego or Self? 68
Nothing, If Not Critical 71
Crater in the Soul 74

Reluctant... to Stop 78
Committed to Self-Destruction 80
Tyranny of Perfection 84
Clinging to Case 90
Behind the Barricade 93
Betrayed 97
Going Robot 99
Poised for Outrage! 101
Shadow 105
Self! Righteous! 107
Walled Inside 109
Problem: Summary 112
Section 3: Solution 115
Solution: Overview 116
What If? 118
What's Holosophy? 120
What's a Holon? 123
Breaking Free 125
Changing Minds 127
Best Answer 131
Brain *Receives* Mind 135
Out of Our Minds 140
3 Kinds of Mind 143
Cognitive Optimization 149
Experience? or Engram? 153
The Transformative Dialogue 156
Counsel/Tutorial 159
Erasure 161
Counseling—Holding the Space 163
Opening Questions 166
Mind as Lens 168
Solution: Summary 170

Section 4: Praxis 173
Praxis: Overview 174
Habits of Practice 176
Catching Your "Self" 180
Shelf Space 183
One Stanza 186
I Won't Trance! 188
The State of Things 191
Talk, Learn, Laugh! 193
The Whole of It! 195
New Awareness 197
Habits of Clarity 199
Ok, Do Me! 201
Assume You're Wrong 203
Indicators 206
Constructing Victimhood 210
Revealed Pretense 212
Looking Out 215
It's Hard! 217
Blame & Resistance 220
A Connection 222
Presence, Choice, Responsibility 224
A Higher Standard 228
The Journey Never Ends 232
Connections 235
Things Change 237
Triple Threat 240
Proof in Praxis 245
Praxis: Summary 248

Section 5: Then... What? 251
Then... What? Overview 252
Home & Holidays 254

Success in a Small Arena	257
Easily Missed	260
Emergence	263
Growing Circles	265
Good, in Greater Quantity	268
Calculus of Optimization	271
I Cannot	273
Keep On	275
Empathy	277
Commit to Discovery	279
Indicators II	281
Finding Truth	285
Truth Functions	288
Hell, Heaven, Here	291
Troubles Come With!	293
The Game	295
What's New?	298
Then... What?: Summary	302
Section 6: Commentary	**305**
Commentary: Overview	306
Another Turn	308
A Culture of Enquiry	310
False Dichotomy?	312
Belief "Systems"	315
Previous Station	317
Not Required	320
Hucksters	322
Move Toward Beauty	324
Bearing Witness	328
The Perfect Tool	331
Into the Mystic	333
Degree of Emergence	337

One, Two, Three! ... 340
The Hidden Good ... 342
One You ... 344
Wider Perspective ... 348
What, Again? ... 350
Birthing Our Future ... 352
Fundamental Non-Local ... 355
Maybe ... 357
One's Own Truth ... 359
Chop Wood. Carry Water! ... 361
There's Time ... 363
Spiritual, Obviously! ... 364
The Long Road ... 366
Puzzles ... 368
Commentary: Summary ... 371
Section 7: End ... 373
End: Overview ... 374
Defending Our Delusions ... 376
Holosophy's Character ... 378
No "Robe" Required ... 380
Altitude ... 382
Not the Teacher ... 384
Robert Thomas ... 387
Return to Foley's Hill ... 389
Start at the Center ... 391
J. R. (Jennifer) StJohn ... 394

Book Map

Holosophy®
Conquering Your Fear of Success

BookMap®

Using this Book	viii
Foley's Hill	ix
Invitation to a Dialogue	xi
Book Map	1
Section 1: Preface	**3**
Welcome	4
Give and Take	6
New Words	8
Colophon	10
Who Needs Holosophy?	11
Mere Survival?	14
Closer to Fine	16
Change the World	18
Summary: Enlarged Perspective	22

Section 2: Problem	**25**
Problem: Overview	26
Never Again!	29
Post-Traumatic Stress	34
Sequester	37
Dirty Lens	40
Lessons Learned	45
Habitual Perception	49
Armor Against Loss	53
Redundant Reflexive Memory	55
Tendrils of Trauma	58
Mechanism of Interference	61
What We Never Question	64
Ego or Self?	68
Nothing, If Not Critical"	71
Crater in the Soul	74
Reluctant... to Stop	78
Committed to Self-Destruction	80
Tyranny of Perfection	84
Clinging to Case	90
Behind the Barricade	93
Betrayed	97
Going Robot	99
Poised for Outrage!	101
Shadow	105
Self Righteous!	107
Walled Inside	109
Problem: Summary	112

Section 3: Solution	**115**
Solution: Overview	116
What If?	118
What's Holosophy?	120
What's a Holon?	123
Shelf Space	125
Breaking Free	127
Changing Minds	131
Best Answer	135
Brain Receives Mind	140
Out of Our Minds	143
3 Kinds of Mind	149
Cognitive Optimization	153
Experience? or Engram?	156
The Transformative Dialogue	159
Counsel/Tutorial	161
Erasure	163
Counseling—Holding the Space	166
Opening Questions	168
Mind as Lens	170
Solution: Summary	

Section 4: Praxis	**173**
Praxis: Overview	174
Habits of Practice	176
Catching Your "Self"	180
Shelf Space	183
One Stanza	186
I Won't Trance!	188
The State of Things	191
Talk, Learn, Laugh!	193
The Whole of It!	195
New Awareness	197
Habits of Clarity	199
Ok, Do Me!	201
Assume You're Wrong	203
Indicators	206
Constructing Victimhood	210
Revealed Pretense	212
Looking Out	215
It's Hard!	217
Blame & Resistance	220
A Connection	222
Presence, Choice, Responsibility	224
A Higher Standard	228
The Journey Never Ends	232
Connections	235
Things Change	237
Triple Threat	240
Proof in Praxis	245
Praxis: Summary	248

Section 5: Then... What?	**251**
Then... What? Overview	252
Home & Holidays	254
Success in a Small Arena	257
Easily Missed	260
Emergence	263
Growing Circles	265
Good, in Greater Quantity	268
Calculus of Optimization	271
I Cannot	273
Keep On	275
Empathy	277
Commit to Discovery	279
Indicators II	281
Finding Truth	285
Truth: Functions	288
Hell, Heaven, Here	291
Troubles Come With!	293
The Game	295
What's New?	298
Then... What?: Summary	302

Section 6: Commentary	**305**
Commentary: Overview	306
Another Turn	308
A Culture of Enquiry	310
False Dichotomy?	312
Belief "Systems"	315
Previous Station	317
Not Required	320
Hucksters	322
Move Toward Beauty	324
Bearing Witness	328
The Perfect Tool	331
Into the Mystic	333
Degree of Emergence	337
One, Two, Three!	340
The Hidden Good	342
One You	344
Wider Perspective	348
What, Again?	350
Birthing Our Future	352
Fundamental Non-Local	355
Maybe	357
One's Own Truth	359
Chop Wood, Carry Water!	361
There's Time	363
Spiritual, Obviously!	364
The Long Road	366
Puzzles	368
Commentary: Summary	371

Section 7: End	**373**
End: Overview	374
Defending Our Delusions	376
Holosophy's Character	378
No "Robe" Required	380
Altitude	382
Not the Teacher	384
Robert Thomas	387
Return to Foley's Hill (Summary)	389
Start at the Center	391
J. R. (Jennifer) StJohn	394

The Holosophy Foundation

Holosophy - Conquering Your Fear of Success   1

Section 1: Preface

Welcome

"Let me tell you why you're here.
You're here because you know something.
What you know you can't explain, but you feel it.
You've felt it your entire life, that there's something wrong with the world. You don't know what it is, but it's there, like a splinter in your mind, driving you mad. It is this feeling that has brought you to me.
Do you know what I'm talking about? I didn't say it would be easy.
I just said it would be the truth."
—**Morpheus** — *The Matrix*

Have the quotes touched a nerve — not quite gone numb? That sense of dull upset, of feeling short-changed by life? The consideration that there's more: if you just knew how to access it?

We felt the same unease in Church, at University, at Work — hoping to discover where the actual meaning might have been hidden... so we continued to search.

And we found each other, and "the Perennial Wisdom" — that great pathway of ancient knowledge, leading inexorably to this moment — where you are poised to begin a new journey — toward that "still higher perch."

There's lots to learn, much to re-affirm and a great deal to acquire. But it's up to you. Soon, you'll be moving up, and someday guiding others as they tread the ancient stair — "Up, always Up!"

So, it begins.

Give and Take

"Think like a wise man but communicate in the language of the people."
—**William Butler Yeats**

Philosophy (the love and study of wisdom) is hard, and deep. It lives, stealthily embedded just under the surface in our daily actions, thoughts and dreams.

But unfortunately, most of us don't go in there very often, so it's unfamiliar country. (Even the word is somehow, a little scary...)

So let's have this conversation; but let's speak mostly in plain language not in the jargon of professional philosophers.

Let's "give voice" not just to the words and hopes of the teacher, but also to the doubts, fears, criticisms and curiosities which prompt the student to reach out for an answer. This is a Teaching Interchange — a long-term conversation with many goals:

To solve one's personal problems.

To acquire wisdom.

To build upon what has gone before and enhance the wisdom tradition for a new century.

This manuscript is formatted as a series of questions and answers between student and teacher... in a classical Call & Response fashion.

The first section of a chapter will usually reflect the thinking, fears, suspicions, criticisms, language, doubts and attempted solutions of the student. The second portion reflects the Master's answer, and the larger Holosophy perspective addressing the subject.

There's no road where we're going. We may have to search for the best path, and decide to leave another for next time. We may have to retrace our steps from time to time.

And, bless you; of course you can teach it faster and better for those who follow after you! And so you must!

New Words

"All words are pegs to hang ideas on."
—Henry Ward Beecher

Holosophy seems to require a new vocabulary. Is it really necessary?

Holosophy uses the English language as a tool to introduce a new perspective about human and spiritual development. Some of our work re-organizes and re-conceptualizes the work of others; so we can use the language as it exists to reference these ideas. So far, so good.

Much of our work, however, introduces ideas and practices which are, well; new. So we have had to coin some new words, and use *old* words in *new* ways to indicate a new and different path, a next step in the great stairway of the Perennial Philosophy.

Throughout history, new ideas and new practices have

generally required a new vocabulary, to indicate a new way of thinking.

Just to be clear, we've created a new approach to spiritual discipline, called Holosophy, a new way of referring to the individual source point behind a human being called the Holon, a new name for the life force itself called Holos; and new terms for the disciplines involved in spiritual development: Cognitive Optimization, The Transformative Dialogue and the Calculus of Optimization.

Our colophon (publisher's mark) is colorful, light-hearted and represents not only the multiple domains of a whole life, but the Holosophy Foundation as well.

It takes time to get acquainted with new ideas. One has to wrestle with the new words and the ideas they represent. One has to hold them up to the light and see them clearly, then try them out in discussion with friends and colleagues. One has to get in the arena and argue a little bit. Eventually, one has to apply and engage with these new ideas to see if they produce a moment (or more) of clarity and shed some light on the age-old challenge of emergence.

Welcome to the arena.

Colophon

Noun: A Publisher's Mark, as in branding thru symbology

In the unconscious, instantaneous Calculus of Optimization, the human being manifests an unparalleled ability to work an eight-level equation while at the same time breathing, singing, cooking, eating or making love. Leave aside writing a play or simply working the posture "Part the Wild Horse's Mane"... It's a little daunting — if one has to think about it... Then you catch yourself thinking, and smile...
- Holosophy Elder

Life: It's "Calculus in Constant Motion." The moment you put aside one area of interest, another presents itself for consideration, then another. Fortunately, we're good at it. We do it unconsciously — even, and especially, while having fun.

That's why the Colophon is such a perfect symbol for the multi-layered, ongoing, infinite process of human interaction — at its best.

The colors indicate the interpenetrating nature of the eight life domains — one blends instantly and seamlessly into another. With the reality of each constantly evolving in its own sphere and simultaneously interacting with all the others...

Choosing a symbol to represent Holosophy, this emerging, evolving step in the Perennial Wisdom is no small task, but we think The Colophon will do nicely...

Who Needs Holosophy?

"You cannot teach a man anything.
You can only help him to discover it within himself."
—Galileo Galilei

As it turns out, a lot of people can benefit, as Holosophy identifies the unrecognized source of many personal barriers, codifies the practices and techniques for removing them, and explores a path for further growth — as desired.

No drugs, no trance, no dogma. Just an ongoing dialogue between Counselor and Client.

If you're alive, and you have a past, you can probably use Holosophy.

Two reasons:

1. Relief

All of us have had some tough times, which leave a bad taste, overhanging our day-to-day life. Our natural human response to difficulty is to remember such times with a terrible intensity — ceaselessly re-creating them so as "never to experience that again!" At some point, those ever-present tense memories tend to overpower our ability to function in the present. "Compulsively re-creating every tense moment from the past" sooner or later starts to bleed off portions of the limited store of available attention. Releasing the stress from those memories allows you to focus on the present and the future with greater intensity — and pleasure.

2. Expansion

Maybe you're doing just fine! You've got it made! Everything still works! Except, you haven't considered how to expand or improve your life, your personal perspective, your family, your career, your community, let alone your people, your connection with other living things, the environment or with the arts or the life of the mind and spirit.

We suggest that there's more than just making enough money and sitting pretty.

For some lucky people, the barrier isn't to surviving, but to getting on with thriving!

Maybe not everyone needs Holosophy. But if you want to let something go, or bring something new into being, it might be worthwhile to begin from a whole new, loftier perspective!

Mere Survival?

"Is that all there is?"
"If that's all there is my friends, then let's keep dancing.
Let's break out the booze and have a ball
If that's all there is..."
Music & Lyrics: **Mike Stoller, Jerry Leiber**
C: Sony/ATV Tunes
Performed by **Peggy Lee**, 1969

Is that it? Getting a job (with a solid base, three weeks vacation), a house and acquiring stuff? As you look around, many people live that model — struggle for their education, find a job, obtain safe living quarters, procreate; then fall asleep — with the occasional argument about food, sex or finances...

But maybe there's more… Consider that the world is your oyster.

Keep searching and learning, discover your purpose and rise to meet the challenge of changing your planet, your culture, your family, your community and yourself for the better.

Perhaps there's more to life than mere survival.

Maybe you can raise the bar?

Closer to Fine

"I went to the doctor, I went to the mountains
I looked to the children, I drank from the fountain
There's more than one answer to these questions
Pointing me in a crooked line
The less I seek my source for some definitive
The closer I am to fine."
Closer To Fine
—**The Indigo Girls**

The "dis-quiet of the spirit" is at the center (yet deeply under the surface) of life. Everyone has it, yet few talk about it. The great religions were begun as answers to this churning, wandering quest for answers to the fundamental questions: Who am I really? Why am I here? What is life? What's our purpose? What's my purpose? How am I supposed to be? How should one conduct a life, How do I do it? Does this experience have meaning; What? Why?

Yet, after so many centuries, many of our cultural and religious institutions have begun to repel honest seekers with their encrustations of greed, exclusion, power, control, rent-seeking and all-too-human hierarchy. Then the brave (sometimes desperate) souls strike out again to find their own answers.

Many have been "scammed" by someone promising the answer — in exchange for cash, wordless fealty and lifelong compliance. "It's a business. People on Quests get Taken. That's the deal. Maybe you're one of them, one of us..."

Given the circumstances, it's not unreasonable to be curious, hungry and suspicious all at once.

> "There is only one religion,
> though there may be a hundred versions of it."
> **—George Bernard Shaw**

The search is as old as human kind — reaching for answers (in and to) the infinite. Along the way, a lot of ideas and approaches have been explored and discarded. Some have been found useful, even rewarding. Those have been retained (etched as steps in the upward stairway...) in the form of the Perennial Wisdom. We think Holosophy is a significant addition. Holosophy doesn't have the answers, but we can help you find your own; with new perspective, practices and community.

Together, we can get closer to fine.

Change the World

"Everyone thinks to change the world.
But nobody thinks to change themselves!"
—Leo Tolstoy

"We can change the world, rearrange the world.
It's dying to get better!"
—Graham Nash

Examine Your Habits: of Thought, of Word, of Deed, because all meaningful change starts right at the center of the individual.

The magic is not out there. It's in here!

And it's in here where you'd never think to look. Your habits — of thought, of speech, of action. For many (if not most) human beings, their unexamined habits camouflage a truck-full of damaging and self-defeating perspectives and behaviors.

Ever been remorselessly and "justifiably" critical of everyone else on the freeway during your commute? Every day? Going and coming? Imagine, all those commuters, all detesting everyone else on the road, all jousting, all cooking in their collective juice. And all considering that everyone else is somehow less-than-human and deserving of annihilation. If we're all like that, like you, what?

We're of the opinion that change (cognitions, new moments of awareness) begins at home. It's our all-too-human tendency to habitually and unconsciously harbor hostile ideas, negative considerations and levels of criticality which ultimately bring about our own downfall.

Consider: What if nobody else does it to us? What if We do it to ourselves?

Try that on as a working hypothesis, and take a look inside...

Is there any criticality in there? Any long-held upsets, treasured since childhood? Sure we keep our wins close to our breast, but isn't there an ancient loss that still seems unjustified — and a miscreant somewhere out there in the world — who hasn't yet paid the price for leaving our desire for revenge un-fulfilled?

How much space is taken up in your mind, keeping those ancient upsets on the shelf? What degree of free energy might you bring to bear on life-in-this-moment if you unloaded all that pent-up history? All the fears, all the "must proves," all the reasons you treasure for not getting up and changing your existence?

Here's a final consideration:

What if all that criticism, doubt, fear, internal holding-on to an upset — all of it, is with great subtlety, still energized and radiating its own world view — even though you've pushed it onto the back shelf? Wow... Nobody knows what you harbor in your inner spaces. But what if everything you've left unresolved is still in there — thinking — and still influencing the flavor of your daily life.

So clean house, and catch yourself — on the freeway perhaps... If you're not sending out good vibrations, what are you sending?

We can Change the World. Starting right here.

Does this work?

1. For You:

Take a look. Do you find yourself flipping in and out of the present as you reference your considerations about how today's circumstances prove and fit with your pre-conceived notions of "how things are?" Does it help? The Freeway, the lunch counter, the security check-in.

2. For the Family:

Have you unconsciously ascribed certain features to your partner, your kids, your siblings? Do you check your memories to find out "How Uncle Don is about women..." before giving him room to meet the attractive new neighbor? What if you and the rest of the family leave the preconceptions at home?

3. The Office:

Is there a person nobody likes? Is there good reason? Can you change that by starting a fresh thread and leaving the old stuff out of the daily interchange?

We can change the world. We suggest that daily life is an endless process of re-creation-in-every-second.

It's dying (and being reborn) to get better!

Summary: Enlarged Perspective

"I've got vision, while the rest of the world uses bifocals...."
—**Butch Cassidy** in *Butch Cassidy & the Sundance Kid*

The great benefit of Holosophy is a widened, lengthened, deepened and enlarged perspective about what life is, how it can be seen, undertaken and lived.

I remember being amazed at how my Father patiently explained to me how to deal with school, my mates, my challenges. He saw more deeply than I.

My teachers along the way all saw more than I, because they looked into life for things I didn't know existed.

Partly, it's experience. But experience alone doesn't give you the depth of perception that training and practice together provide.

Most people simply don't look at life as a spiritual journey, not as a game, not as uniquely responsive to individual initiative and intention. They don't know much about their own body/mind/spirit structure, because they simply haven't looked or questioned. Their perspective is fundamentally limited by the fact that they can't see clearly what's happening all around them. Their vision is occluded by their experiences. They know all about life, but they haven't seen it clearly.

They haven't found teachers, because it never occurred to them that such teachers existed, or that there might be something more to be learned.

Holosophy's greatest service may be in its contribution of indicating and removing barriers to insight. When you choose to expand your range of vision, you can see both **more**, and more **clearly**. When you can see more clearly, there's no limit to what you might perceive.

Section 2: Problem

Success Reluctance

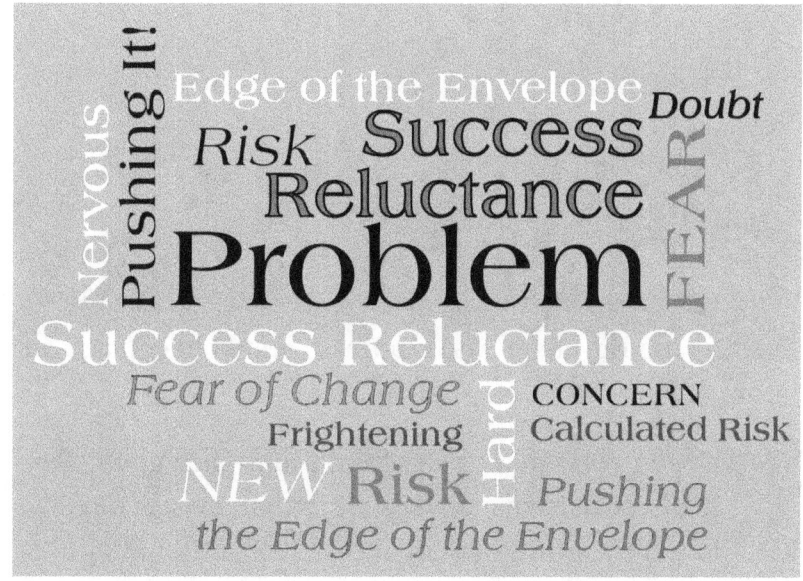

Problem: Overview

"There are old test pilots.
And bold test pilots.
There are few old, bold test pilots."
— **Chuck Yeager, USAF**
First to Break the Sound Barrier

"Pushing the Envelope" was a phrase created to explain the nature of flying experimental aircraft.

The point was to fly faster than usual, then go higher than usual, to maneuver harder than ever before; to test the limits of pilot and aircraft. After all, in combat, the plan is to deliberately "push the edge," while forcing one's opponent to go beyond, make a mistake and presumably, to crash.

The phrase, with its air-combat derring-do became popular, if not well understood, and has slowly faded from everyday conversation. But the underlying concept: "the bargain we strike in search of success" is as **common as the day's headlines. It's clear in all cultures that the Price of Success is Risk.** Business is all about risks and rewards; but academia, medicine, statecraft, the arts, literature and family life all require that one "place a wager" from time to time, and put one's reputation, fortune, safety, self-confidence, affection or maybe life itself — on the line.

Risk and a fuller life seem to go hand in hand.

But this book isn't about real risks. It is instead about our Fear of Risk and our tendency to retreat not only from the real thing, but from anything that looks, sounds, feels or even reminds us of risk. And of course, if we retreat from risk, we also retreat from success. Hence the phrase, Success Reluctance.

Success Reluctance is not an obvious malady, because it is invisible, deeply hidden beneath the level of conscious awareness. It looks like nothing, because it is nothing. Not a clear and present danger, but an unclear and camouflaged fear of everything required to succeed. **Engagement on the field, the idea of contest, confronting the challenge, growth, movement, change — all are required for success, and all re-stimulate the hidden fears of individuals, races, nations, and human kind.**

But what wonders might we create if we become fully aware of our submerged, invisible fears and reluctance? Could we not engage life more fully; and reach out, even to the stars?

The remainder of this chapter summarizes many of the

ways Success Reluctance subtly and for the most part un-noticed, manifests in the day-to-day lives of people who appear so normal as to defy categorization. Success Reluctance is an unconscious, interior phenomenon, which nudges its victim not to participate, not to stand and deliver, not to speak up, not to turn out, not to reach, not to experiment, not to move, but to wait for the urge to pass. It looks like nothing, and it creates nothing. It simply prevents virtually any and every move toward the new.

Becoming aware of this unconscious and insidious tendency is the first step to moving forward.

Are we suggesting that you "put the hammer down" and rush, unthinking into battle? Of course not! But as you become aware of your (irrational) reluctance to risk, you can then address it more thoughtfully—and with full awareness, consciously **push the envelope** by choice.

Never Again!

"A cat who sits on a hot stove top, will never sit on a hot stove top again.
And that is well.
But she will never sit on a cold one either."
—Mark Twain

I'm a happy, successful business consultant. I live in New York, and travel on business.

I'm in my thirties, feeling confident that I know how to move my life along the path to my next stop. I have a great condominium, pay my

> taxes, have an active social life and enjoy a variety of entertainment and social diversions. I've left the church over "the Rules!" I guess you could say "I'm Spiritual, Not Religious."
>
> A friend told me about Holosophy and I'm curious… (Who isn't interested in how to improve?) But while I'm curious, I feel like I might not be a good candidate… I mean, I AM successful!
>
> OK, well that's not entirely true… I do have some challenges with my family. And there is that issue about being taken seriously by the Boss. I tend to get a little nervous when I go to the MD for labs and samples, so I push that off as long as I can. And I dream about a trip to Nepal, but I have not actually planned a date. As to the future, I wish I could meet a partner who meets my standards, but most people are just not right.
>
> So maybe I have a few issues…

Yeah, you really messed that up! It was understandable, of course. You were young, and aggressive and knew it all. But some people got hurt, and there's that earlier marriage. That failed business undertaking. And those kids.

So you pulled up stakes and put it behind you. Decided "Never to do that again!"

The behavior was wrong and damaging. But the subsequent decision, while practical, perhaps, carried the freight of absoluteness. A "good" decision, carried the added burden of a "never!"

You were Right, Then. And There! But Now, there's a new challenge... New circumstances, people, job. A whole different gig. And here you are — smart, experienced, seasoned; hungry to contribute — bursting to use your combined experience and make things better.

And. Nothing.

You're standing here poised — and stopped. Because you've decided to never make that mistake again — not ever! So everyone is waiting for your contribution, looking at you. It's your time. You can make this better. You can. You know you can. You've seen how this plays out. But you're frozen. Not out of lack of understanding; but because of your own decision never to risk anything like that again.

Well. So much for the benefit of experience. We call it "Success Reluctance." Naturally, any genuine success is not accomplished without risk. At the sub-rational level of understanding, that small risk cascades into a series of small steps forward, and two in retreat. Avoiding a repeat of that early mistake is all that matters to this way of thinking. So *it* succeeds, while *you* fail. The early failure is *not* repeated, but the big new success *never* has a chance.

Interesting how our early experiences of having "done harm or gotten hurt" may keep us from doing it again, but also keep us from growing or helping. In a funny way, what was wrong then and there, keeps you from doing what's right here and now! Ring up another loss, as the process continues.

Success Reluctance: something that is present but almost unnoticed in every life. The thing about Success Reluctance, is that it *feels* like Success...

This ongoing dwindling spiral continues until we arrest the process through dialogue, then begin to re-examine our assumptions, premises and constructs to start fresh in the here and now!

Are your old, safe limits holding you back from a new and better level of achievement?

Applications

1. For You

Have you found a good Counselor? Not one who says: "How do you feel about that?" But one who helps you dig out the assumptions, resolutions and premises you created based on a moment of failure in a dark time... That requires some detective teamwork; but once you see it, the re-integration can happen instantly! Find good counsel. We all need it.

2. At Home:

Have you and your partner been through some tough times? Made any firm assumptions or resolutions based on that tough experience? Are they still valid — after all these years? Maybe it's time to pause and lay down the firm foundation for life going forward. After all, you've changed!

3. At Work:

Is your last boss the one that bit you? Are you giving *this* one a wide berth without good reason? Are you keeping four cylinders on idle because you think it's too risky to excel? How's that working for you?

You sure don't want to do *that* again! That much hurt, that much damage... But why not take all that experience and give today's family, neighborhood and workplace the entire benefit of all you know?

You may have been Wrong in the Past, but make sure to be Right going forward!

Post-Traumatic Stress

"You can't patch a wounded soul with a Band-Aid."
—**Michael Connelly**, The Black Echo

Well the title says it all! There *was* a trauma. But there *is* stress. And the stress *continues*...

That's the hang-up isn't it? The trauma is over and in the past, but the stress continues and recurs in the present. Again and again. People find themselves physically healed from the injury, but anytime something "triggers" them, they are immediately cast back to the moment of that traumatic event. Maybe it's a sound, maybe a smell, maybe a face, a voice, a breeze — a trigger.

The Warriors are our Cultural Educators about what happens to us in extremis.

When dark damaging things happen, we retain not only a clear and rational memory, but also a redundant, muddy, dark, occluded, stress-infused, memory of the trauma. And that event/memory just won't die. It becomes an encoded, submerged part of the individual; hidden from view; gathering substance as we build our resistance to it, and waiting to spring into being when triggered.

It's our engineering. We apparently consider some events so powerful, threatening and life-arresting that we soak up everything in an instant of pain, stress, upset or trauma and keep a redundant copy, just in case — forever.

That would not be a problem in itself, but for the multiplicity of chance triggers. Research tells us that the number of potential trigger items is almost limitless. Any *indicator* the mind can recall, may also become a *trigger* if it happens in proximity to the traumatic event. The mind simply "grabs" everything about the event and files it away as what we label Sub-Rational Information. We're not fully aware of it. It's not really about thinking, but about reacting and rejecting this current circumstance because it looks, sounds or feels similar to that earlier moment. It's not really rational, but instead a knee jerk, fight or flight reflex that can reduce a fully capable human being to a hollow mockery of his normal warrior self. Repeatedly.

These Sub-Rational memories and their triggers, are the subjects and the objects of the Transformative Dialogue.

While the concept of PTSD is most prominent and public among "warrior types," the syndrome is much more widely spread than previously recognized. One doesn't necessarily have to be in a life and death gun battle in order to encounter a sufficient level of stress or emotional trauma to initiate the sub-rational response. Many ordinary life experiences, (a traffic accident, an illness, a breakup or divorce, a trip to the hospital, a fall from a horse, a sports injury) can create enough stress and emotional recoil to initiate the formation of redundant records. "PTS" is not so much limited to heroes, as it is a regular part of a full life.

Sequester

"Most men resemble great deserted palaces: the owner occupies only a few rooms and has closed off wings where he never ventures."
—**François Mauriac**, writer, Nobel laureate

Sequester [si-kwes-ter] verb (used with object)

1. to remove or withdraw into solitude or retirement; seclude.

2. to remove or separate; banish; exile.

3. to keep apart from others; segregate or isolate:

"The jury was sequestered until a verdict was reached."

But I am equally tough. I decided that a tough life would not defeat me!

My solution: Sequester.

It works for all the tough subjects and people!

I just "Wall Off" all the ugly aspects of life, the difficult family issues, the mean holiday gatherings, the hard career issues. Then,

> having "tied off" and compartmentalized all the difficult things, I work like hell with the time and energy I have left, and create my own brand of Success Against All Odds. I put the bad stuff in locked-down locations in my mind, and I live, work and practice in the remaining (safe) space where the bad stuff never shows.
>
> Admittedly, it has its downside... Pictures of my family no longer appear in my presence — to say nothing of my actual family.
>
> I don't discuss (or think about) my previous religious perspective with anyone, ever.
>
> Politics is definitely out, and after that stuff with my Coach, no sports.
>
> All neatly walled off and hidden in the high-pressure zone that is my Sequester area.
>
> But look at me! I am a winner! In spite of everything.

Who can argue? But just imagine what you might accomplish without that five hundred pound weight around your neck.

We experience something awful. And, being infinitely capable beings, we "wall off that event, that day, or that entire period" and continue to function as well as possible in the rest of our life.

"It's always there." But we function in spite of it! And that is a victory — such as it is...

"Sequestration"

It's a great strategy for "compartmentalizing the damage." It says a lot about our capabilities that we continue to reach, create and grow in spite of the sometimes harsh circumstances handed to us. They do not destroy us, but merely slow us down.

Holosophy sees this from a slightly different viewpoint: that of repair, reinstatement and re-ensoulment. We suggest that it's not necessary to retreat entirely from life when hurt; but to pause and reflect; while harvesting "the wisdom in the lesson;" then moving back into the area of damage as a larger, stronger, wiser individual.

Sequestration is a perfectly normal response to damage; to resolve, "Well, I'll never go back there again!" A family confrontation can leave a person concluding that it is best to retire from the arena during holiday periods and come out only when the potential for ongoing contact and its attendant upsets has been minimized. "Sequestered from November through February and other holidays." We reach for simple, if minimal workability, and succeed; while yet falling something short of actual wholeness...

Holosophy counsels the alternative: that hurt can be healed, that pain can be substantially forgotten, that damage can be repaired. And that we are better for it. But we have to knock down the walls, step out of the closet, rise to the challenge of confronting whatever happened; and getting on with life — without that enormous weight.

Yes! You're amazing! Sequestration, though, is at best, a temporary solution. It shouldn't become a lifetime policy.

Dirty Lens

"Your assumptions are your windows on the world.
Scrub them off every once in a while,
or the light won't come in."
—Alan Alda

"The fault, dear Brutus, lies not in our stars, but in ourselves."
—William Shakespeare

I've been pretty successful in my life so far...

I know how to succeed in the job. Work is about impressing the boss, so you can get ahead. I've gotten pretty good about knowing what she wants and getting it for her, quick.

I know how to get along with others, just line up with the leader of the group, and keep to their line of thinking!

I was poor while growing up, I'll never be poor again! My mantra is get busy and make

> some scratch!
>
> I haven't met my mate yet, but it'll be great! I'll be successful, rich, in with the right people and on my way!
>
> As to religion, I always thought that charity stuff was for the birds. So when I saw the Deacon helping himself from the collection plate, I knew for sure that deal was a scam!
>
> So Holosophy... What can you do for a Winner like me?

Seen through a dirty window, a sunny day looks gray, dark and dim. So, not willing to tolerate a less than accurate view, we clean the window.

Our individual "point of view" on the world (which we often mistake for ourselves...) is not necessarily pristine or unalterable. Sometimes, we collect a little dust or a smudge on the lens in the form of an attitude that tends to show up only around certain people. Maybe it's a way of thinking about someone you "instinctively" dislike... (Instinctively? Really?) Perhaps there's a lack of confidence when facing certain activities. "You know how it's going to turn out, so why go?" Time for a window cleaning?!

Assumptions are the "dirt on the lens" of life. They cloud our view of reality. There's Reality — and "our assumptions" about it. There's Life — and our Beliefs about Life. There's that office meeting you were called to, and there's your hypothesis about its purpose or outcome. And each of those is the creation of a mind — peering through a viewpoint — unaware of the dirt: the beliefs, assumptions and hypotheses which are distorting the perception of what's actually going on.

The accretion of "dirt on the lens", the accumulation of beliefs, assumptions, judgements, doubts, hypotheses, fears, worries; is an un-noticed part of living. It wouldn't be so problematic if we noticed every "bug" on our windshield — for we'd obviously stop and wipe it clean at the next opportunity. But "dirt on the lens of life" collects, (sometimes forever) without our conscious awareness, and so, over time, we are handicapped by our self-imposed disconnection and distancing from life.

Cognitive Optimization: Correcting Our Perceptions

The fault is not in the world, but our perception of it. So it lies with us to optimize our perception, our ability to perceive what is actually occurring, and to respond in ways which are more and more lofty and causative — rather than merely reacting.

The Transformative Dialogue is a Conversation, but a very special one.

You and the counselor; in search of hidden, unconscious assumptions, one life domain at a time. Each time you unearth another assumption (sometimes some very old ones) there's a pause, and a giggle as the old issue clears off. What do you do, when an incorrect assumption comes to light? Right, you smile (sometimes ruefully), thump your forehead and say; "Wow! I had really forgotten that!" So now, lighter, and brighter, you go about your day. No dirt on the Lens, nothing clouds your clear view of the world.

Applications

1. For You

How much dirt is sitting on your lens — un-noticed? Are there any assumptions occluding your clear view of people, circumstances, family or business? Are there some recurring aggravations, irritations, setbacks or upsets that seem to be a standard part of your life experience? Is it possible that they arrived with you? Why not take some time and have a dialogue to engage the examination and clean the lens — before any new problems occur?

2. In the Family

We like our viewpoints. We've grown used to seeing the world through the shaded, shaped and muddied viewpoints to which we've grown so accustomed. Is your son tending to be a bit of a victim from day to day? Does your daughter bully other children? Is your mate/partner sort of dim when it comes to tracking (and being compassionate about) what others think/feel? Have they cleaned their windshields lately? Can you coach them to pay more attention?

3. In the Office

Entire companies, divisions and individual offices are often "stuck in a loss, or stuck in a win." The challenge for you and your team is to keep each other sharp by challenging the cherished assumptions on which you base your day-to-day conduct of the business. Has anything changed? Should it? Must it change in order to foster the emergence of a new success? So?

If your life looks anything other than clear, sharp and distinct, (and optimistic), don't let that cave you in!

Stop, clean the windshield (and your viewpoint) and take another look!

Lessons Learned
(Too Well)

"A censor is seated inside me now. He is testing every word that is born within me. His constant caution that a word may be misunderstood so, or it may be interpreted thus, is a real bother.
But I'm unable to shake him off."
—**Perumal Murugan**

Recent interest in Perumal Murugan's work has exploded, with five novels coming out, translated into English from the original Tamil. After undergoing a vicious attack by caste leaders in his home state of Tamil Nadu, his novel "One Part Woman" was the subject of a landmark court decision defending the right of artists to critically depict their own communities. But Mr. Murugan remains so horrified by the collective punishment meted out to him in his hometown over his book, that he barely speaks about it, even to friends. He doubts he will ever again write about small towns with the same unblinking realism.
—*New York Times:* August 22, 2016

Well OK, I know I should look both ways before crossing the street...

Holosophy - Conquering Your Fear of Success

> And I should probably get to know someone a little bit before getting married and running away to a Greek Island.
>
> But these issues are just "common care", aren't they?
>
> Unless you're trying to tell me there's something more than simply "being careful..."
>
> Wait... Is there a mechanism working in the background?
>
> Something I can't quite see?
>
> Something that I'm not usually aware of, day to day?
>
> That's a little spooky. And maybe worth looking into...

So you've got a life going on. On the surface, there's lots of activity: seeing, participating, reacting, creating... But slightly beneath the surface, there's a part of the mind watching and thinking all the time. It's just a little unconscious... You're not always aware of it, but it's forever making judgements, drawing conclusions, putting things together and seeing connections and creating relationships. Always.

And while all this information gets digested, the data points involved are cross-referenced to create a multi-dimensional web of connections between events, thoughts, ideas and considerations. That whiff of perfume whisks you back to the first time you experienced it. That trumpet concerto sends you on an instant memory trip.

It's something almost beyond understanding, because everything you know gets cross-referenced against everything else — instantly. Lessons Learned.

Fine! This is a good thing! It's how we learn, how we recall and how we connect the dots of life for our own growth and benefit. Until stress comes into the picture.

When we're stressed, however, all that recording and storage power gets turned on "Full!" Every aspect of what happens in a stressful event gets filed — twice: First, as a regular, rational memory. Second, as a Sub-Rational event; co-mingled and cross-referenced with all the other stressful moments. Seems like a good idea, but under stress we don't think so clearly — that web of connections becomes hypersensitive and "charged." As a result, if we again experience anything even remotely related to something we experienced before under stress, we tend to get overwhelmed by a flood of similar, but not really germane incidents and information. Stress causes us to file and recall as if we're blind, drunk and illiterate. That's why we call this the "Sub-Rational Mind."

Worse, because of the stress-induced significance of Sub-Rational material, it tends to overwhelm our rational capacities and cause our fight or flight reflexes to kick in... So our Lessons Learned and Conclusions Drawn become very sensitive Lessons Learned Too Well!

Because of this instinctive, habitual defensive cross-referencing, in a very curious way, "Everything New can become Old Again." A chance encounter in the present moment instantly sends us back to an earlier, uglier moment — whether we need it or not. We find ourselves compulsively re-living unhappy moments, lessons and conclusions over and over and our confidence in "facing the new" takes a beating. It's maybe a small glitch in our programming, but it can cause significant problems.

The thinking that creates the Sub-Rational mind takes place almost beneath conscious awareness. But it can be accessed in a quiet moment with a calm, focused attention and the steady, sustained intention to reveal the misapplied cross-referencing that caused the problem in the first place. Another requirement is the patience to confront the sheer magnitude of the web of assembled and cross-referenced memories, considerations and sensory data. You don't take it on all at once, or in a single sitting.

That's the point of the "Transformative Dialogue" in Holosophy. Two people, one who listens, and by their presence guarantees the discussion has to take place in an objective format — outside the mind, in the shared space. You can't easily be shanghaied by the Sub-Rational mind when there's another person present. Together, you take up the examination of the areas you deem most important, and one at a time, work through them until the added pressure and significance granted under stress is released. Sub-Rational gives way to Rational.

Lessons Learned allow us to grow and move into a better future.

But, Lessons Learned too well keep us locked in a walled garden — "safe" from the new.

Habitual Perception

"The real voyage of discovery consists not in seeking new landscapes, but in seeing with new eyes."
—Marcel Proust

"**I** am not what you think I am...
You are what you think I am..."

James was slowly becoming aware of what he didn't have...

The little town he lived in had "everything." On Main Street, there was a "good" restaurant, a drive-up hamburger place, a grocery store and druggist. One street over, there was a county Library by the WPA Field House with a basketball gym, tennis courts and handball courts as well. Everything anyone could ever need. A set of loving parents, some friends on the block. Life was good! Seen through the lens of his life up to "Now," everything was just fine.

Then came High School, and those kids from the other side of the district. They seemed to have nicer clothes, cars, cool stuff, as well as a self-assured cockiness that seemed somehow, out of place but still higher toned than the quiet submission of the kids from "around here." Something had changed, not only out there; but also "in here," in terms of James' habitual ways of seeing things.

The regular Speech Tournaments James attended as a part of the high school team, introduced him to players from around the state and the nation. He became aware of the fact that others had resources he could only dream of or fantasize about, and they also had a confidence — which seemed to radiate out of them like a fine mist. He began to anticipate the way they would meet and then discount him as a competitor once they knew from whence he came. He began to expect the knowing look, the pitying appraisal, the arrogant dismissal, the casual disinterest.

Then, he met a girl. After a few dates, she said; "I really like you. I think you're nice, smart, humble, articulate and cute! But I don't get why you can be so cold and cutting when you meet someone from my part of town. What have I done to you to earn that?"

When you look at a thing, really look at it, it changes. It becomes available to you — more fully. The Transformative Dialogue is based on that fundamental reality. That we spend much of our lives inside a protective shell of habitual perception.

We see ourselves in certain self-serving ways, which serve our larger world view. ("Bosses are mean. The world is a marketplace. Everything's for sale."). What we are mostly unaware of, is that these habitual perceptions are not actually fact, but fiction, spun out of the cotton candy of our pre-conditioned imagination.

And our imaginations create their fictions out of the raw material of our basic world view.

It's as if every person goes out into the world wearing a protective bubble of their own habitual perception. Some of us get into scrapes on the freeway. Some of us encounter a dishonest storekeeper. Some of us find a world of giving, friendly people. We suggest, these experiences are founded in what we are looking for or projecting, and the lenses through which we choose to perceive. ("Yeah, the world was a battlefield today, again! I'm glad I lived through it.")

As we begin to more carefully examine an area of conflict or upset, the intensity of our gaze begins to reveal greater detail — and the larger picture emerges. We discover that perhaps the world is not so hostile as we have imagined: that bosses might be engaged in a great quest; that the marketplace is teeming with people building their dreams.

Every event residing in the Sub-Rational mind is an experience, colored with stress, fear, pain, upset or trauma of some kind — sometimes physical, sometimes emotional. All of these events are experienced "through a glass, and darkly." Though we may not be aware of them at every moment, they are present, and influencing our perceptions and choices unconsciously at all times: "Habits of Perception."

As we engage in the Dialogue, we become incrementally more aware of that Sub-Rational lens, working in the background. As our awareness increases, we discover that our world, seen through a Sub-Rational lens, may not be the *real* world at all. In that moment, the lens, itself is reduced in its magnitude and power.

This is not accomplished in a single blinding flash, but in moment after moment of patient examination.

When you look at it, really look at it, it changes!

Armor Against Loss

"Many who have spent a lifetime in it,
can tell us less of love than the child
that lost a dog yesterday."
—Thornton Wilder

As a boy, they called him Davey.

He lost his dog. Penny — The Protector! She played, ran, guarded, loved and entertained! Hit by a car one day, she was gone when he returned from school.

Love terminated in **Shock and Loss**...

He lost an eye to measles. So began the sweltering summer, of laborious uptown bus trips, culminating in submission to the probes of the Ocularist.

Innocence gave way to wrenching pain, partial

blindness and daily teasing by the boys on the way home from school.

Childhood evaporated in **Shock, Betrayal and Loss**...

Then there was Elmer, the beloved calf on Grandpa's farm. Fed in the stall, played with for endless hours in the corral. Later, a family visit culminated in a beefy dinner where Grandpa announced without ceremony; "That's Elmer on your plate there, boy. Enjoy!"

Love gave way to **Shock, Loss & Betrayal**...

As a budding High School track star, "Dave" showed promise as a sprinter. His spikes and Letter Sweater were talismans. Girls began to notice...

Then a mystery illness, and a year off to recover ended the phenom's progress.

Love, Shock, Loss, & Betrayal!

A Pattern emerged, and a Coping Strategy: "Keep Love at a Distance!" to fend off Betrayal, Shock & Loss. Such is the nature of the Sub-Rational Mind, and its role as the "Storehouse of Pain."

Redundant Reflexive Memory

You know how it works. You remember everything. That time on the baseball field, you were running for second and dove for the base, but that other player also had an eye on getting there before you.

Well, you collided. It HURT! You lost consciousness.

But you didn't lose awareness. While you weren't on top of your game as they rushed you to the hospital, you were still aware, beneath the level of conversation or interaction. There you were, the center of attention and tracking everything that happened, from a less-than-conscious point of view.

You tracked and filed away the smell of the surgical soap, the faint aroma of aftershave from the ER Tech, the hospital antiseptic, the texture of those sheets and the pressure of the hospital mattress, the awful flickering institutional light, that beeping sound, the television barely audible in the background, whispers from family and friends as they crowded into the room with you, the smell of flowers from the gift shop, the perfectly normal aroma of coffee from the lobby canteen, and the squeak of foam food boxes as friends took nourishment by your bedside. That deep, superior, Doctor's voice. Oh, and that awful background music in the hallway. And the periodic other-worldly voice on the PA; "Code Blue, Code Blue!" All of that, over-layered with fear, doubt, confusion, desperation and the sense of being out of control and unconsciousness.

You regained consciousness, and recovered. Leaving the hospital a few weeks later, you received a clean bill of health, a large bill, and a neck brace which made you popular at school. Unfortunately, you also carried the burden of a truckload of redundant memories.

Of course, you know you were messed up. You consciously remember the experience, and of course, it wasn't up-lifting. But the challenge of the unconscious memories is more sobering. They have a "grip" on you, because they were acquired both while you were unconscious and under stress.

Oh, and your Sub-Rational circuitry also connected the entire experience with prior, similar memories — you know, anything connected with accidents, unconsciousness, hospitals and stress…

That's the mechanism. We remember everything, and the really stressful stuff we remember redundantly, in its own separate sphere.

We call it "Sub-Rational Memory." Because it's not really a "thoughtful or rational process," it connects things on the basis of "similarity." Over time, every stressful moment seems to find a connection to every other stressful moment, and we get nervous about moving forward on any similar initiative because we may have to re-encounter something that was stressful in the past.

It's a built-in feature of the human condition, but it accumulates and finally occludes our ability to think clearly or evolve without hindrance.

Tendrils of Trauma

"You've got to get yourself together.
You've got stuck in a moment
Now you can't get out of it."
—**U2** "Stuck in a Moment"

How is it that we get "stuck in a moment"? One second, we're having a terrific life experience! Starting a new relationship, going to a new place, exploring a new opportunity; and then, without warning, suddenly things turn dark. You just can't martial the enthusiasm for the new person. The business opportunity turns sour. And there's a pall over everything that seems to say, "Go back! It's all going to turn out badly!"

Seen through the lens of a traumatic event from the past, an exciting, new opportunity can ignite a storm of pyramiding fears, confusion and personal insecurities.

Sub-Rational perception permeates life. Not because all

of life is negative, but because of the unique structure of linkages which connect one event or experience to another through "filing by similarities." There's core material; the deep foundation of an individual's trauma. "Tendrils of Similarity" connect **this** event to **that** terrible time. Maybe in the purview of Sub-Rational thinking, the old event and the new event *seem* to connect because they both happened in the presence of holiday music. Perhaps they are connected by location, at a relative's home. Maybe a perfume or a partner's body scent taints an intimate moment and takes the mind back to a failed date.

None of these indicia are "Rational." But by the tortured logic of Sub-Rationality, they are similar, and therefore, the same — dangerous!

How many types of tendril connections are there? Unfortunately, the possible similarities are legion! Time of day, seasonality, day of the week, scent, proximity, sexuality, background noises, familial relationships, school experiences, social interactions, foods, physical trauma, illness; the list continues.

Tendrils can invisibly connect the present moment to an unhappy past, and leave one feeling apprehensive without a logical reason, but still suffering because of a sub-conscious, Sub-Rational link.

Of course, if it were Rational, (or conscious) you wouldn't be feeling or doing it! But you are feeling or doing it nonetheless! Your awareness is obscured in such times, by the power of Sub-Rational perception. So even though it seems "off" somehow, the desire to run is so powerful that it cannot be ignored.

Later, having emerged from the "moment," you look back and shake your head.

"What was that all about?"

At its core, Sub-Rationality, is obvious, dangerous, and relatively clear. But as the core events recede in time, the tendrils of remembrance are softened, diffused and obscured. Yet there they are, waiting; for some innocuous similarity to cue the alarms.

In the aftermath, a new tendril extends itself, invisibly, into the future...

Mechanism of Interference

"Learn how to see. Realize that everything connects to everything else."
—Leonardo Da Vinci

Have you ever met someone, and immediately felt an instant, visceral dislike? Have you entered a stairway in a darkened parking garage and had an eerie sense of unease; turning up your collar and hurrying out of the building?

Ever entered an auditorium and felt a hollow sense of familiarity with the great space, and a sense of something that happened to you in a place just like that?

Ever gotten in the room and felt a presence, which faded on examination? Ever noticed your mind slowing down to sludge during one of those times?

Each in its own way is a manifestation of the Sub-Rational

memory mechanism at work. Something about a place, a person or a circumstance rings a bell with you and yet, you can't pin it down with logic. (It's not logical, just consistent and similar...)

So maybe you can't put a rational spin on this happening, but you've noticed from time to time that you get a message, a perception, that something is up!

If you're still thinking clearly, it's a signal that this is merely a memory... Not a flashback, or a trigger to a state of re-stimulation, just a memory. The process is complex, pervasive and many times, helpful. We can pull up times, places, people and circumstances out of memory just by the sensory data...

But in the darker circumstance, we get a tingle of memory, and we **also** start getting interference... We can't think straight. We're afraid. We're ill. We're frozen; or maybe we run away! Maybe we just stop thinking altogether and even start to lose consciousness. All this is the Sub-Rational Realm on high alert. Many times, our mental lockup in a Sub-Rational moment, will lead us to make a mistake, freeze or otherwise mis-cue and cause another sub-optimum outcome: which promptly gets filed away with all the other data on this line of experience, and the Sub-Rational data continues to accumulate.

The Mechanisms of Memory can be useful and helpful, except when they encounter a particularly difficult, painful or traumatic circumstance. At that point we create duplicates and add the stress, the emotional charge, the overpowering self-preservation information and all recorded data into the same folder. The original (Rational) memory falls into its appointed place, but the duplicate sits, waiting to be "shocked into operation" by the encounter of some scary similarity in real time. Then everything goes phhht!

So the Mechanism of Interference is the same Memory Mechanism we use every day, except for the fact that under stress, the system creates duplicates which clog the system and leave us unable to function when re-triggered.

What We Never Question...

The Ends of the Ham

So I watched as my friend prepared for a ceremonial family dinner. She brought out the ham, cut a couple of inches off both ends, and put them aside. Then, she dressed the ham, covered the pan and put it in the oven to bake. During a pause, I asked her why she cut four inches of perfectly edible meat off both ends of the holiday ham???

She said, "You know, I have no idea, it's the way my mom taught me. Let's ask her!" We moved to the living room and posed the question: "What's the deal with cutting the ends off the ham?"

She got a puzzled look and said, "My mom always did it that way. Let's ask her!" Fortunately, Grandma was on her way to the celebration and joined us later that day. As we helped her remove her coat, and find a seat, the three of us asked about the "Family Ham Recipe." Why do we remove the ends of the ham?

She thought about that for a long time and said, "Well that was a long time ago, but when we first learned how to bake a holiday ham, the hams were too big for the pans, or the ovens! We had to make the ham fit the pan. So we just shortened the ham judiciously, and saved the extra pieces for later..."

> The Self Assured Student
>
> I have gotten pretty far along in my life so far, and I don't mind telling you, I'm a little bit proud and maybe a little confident as well.
>
> I had some challenges growing up, and I overcame them. They're a part of my character now...
>
> So I'm just laying out a challenge here; Teach me. Add to my store of knowledge. Suggest new avenues of thought. Bring me the wisdom of the ages.
>
> Just don't ever, under any circumstances, challenge anything I already know... Especially the stuff I've come to believe is absolutely true! What I know — is true. All right!?
>
> Challenging that, will constitute the end of our relationship.

Consider: Life is made up of the simple building blocks of conclusions we have reached, judgements we have made and come to rely on with certainty over time. Our beliefs may be as close to actually being "us" as anything in the universe. (But of course, they aren't us, are they?) (Believer, or Belief?) Because those beliefs are so close to us, so useful and so ephemeral, we can go a long time without looking at them too closely. And, we **like** those beliefs. We trust them. We rely on them as our operating software. What could possibly go wrong?

When you reach a conclusion under traumatic stress, it tends to stick. It becomes "part of the furniture" of your day-to-day perspective. And, as a result, it, along with all the rest, is beyond question.

Could it be that, as Sub-Rational conclusions and judgements are arrived at when our consciousness is occluded by stress, pain, anxiety and fear, they find their way into the secure vault of our treasured truths about life? If that were true, we'd be busy dealing with life in the moment, and something might reactuate one of those deeply held beliefs. Of course, we'd simply act in accordance with it; never questioning the belief, or the results of our acting on it in the moment.

We'd simply "cut both ends off the ham," without question...

Wow. It's "ours," this belief. It's right there in our mind, like the un-examined wallpaper. But it may contain all kinds of things that don't stand up to examination. Especially under current circumstances.

In practice, a very familiar "glitch" in Cognitive Optimization, is getting caught up in a deeply held, previously unexamined belief, which turns out to have been unconsciously acquired. Like a land mine, it is never seen, and fades into the background, until, under pressure, you put your weight upon it. And BOOM!

As Counselors, we learn to establish a bond with the client, which allows us to assist as they return their interest and curiosity to their inner storehouse of beliefs, customs, certainties and assumptions, along with the willingness to hold everything up to the light of investigation in the current moment to see if it's genuine, or just something acquired while unconscious.

A basic Holosophy Tenet: A fundamental indicator of free, un-compromised reason, is the Willingness to Question Everything! (Especially what we think is sacred.)

Even our most cherished assumptions (another word for "Truth") are subject to changes and evolution as we mature and times change. And though we protest and perhaps drag our feet, we ultimately change with the times and our own maturation, because that's part of being an adult.

But be careful, when something is too sacred to touch, too lofty to consider, too valuable to question, so far beyond analysis and examination, it may be hiding in a shelter of Sub-Rational defenses; bolstered by fear, stress, upset and pain. Those are the "truths" that won't bear the light of inspection.

And they are the ones that ultimately must surrender to reasoned examination.

Ego or Self?

"The ego is your self-image; it is your social mask;
The Ego, however, is not who you really are.
It is the role you are playing. It thrives on approval.
It wants control, and it is sustained by power,
because it lives in fear."
—**Deepak Chopra**

Ego exists to be looked at, appreciated, idolized, modeled, adored, and admired. It is a self-generated, pictorial, emotional replica of you. But it has its own agenda. It exists to create a fiction around the self. In the Ego, you are better, taller, smarter, richer, funnier and more sexually appealing than ever. It's your False Ambassador to the world. It has a lot of performance art going on, in order to burnish the image. It isn't you. "It's a creation, based on you." It keeps you safe, and protects the "franchise."

After all, what could be a better protection for a timeless, space-less, immortal being, than a double — to send out into the world as a representative? Even if someone decimated the ego, on Monday morning, **You** could be back on the job, taking care of business — untouched and unbothered. Quite a creation!

The Self, however, is the silent witness, the non-material conscious entity which does the looking.

You may just be starting to slow down and say, "Hey. Wait! If the "Self" (The Holon) is immortal, non-material, fully and totally conscious, a unique manifestation of conscious awareness; Why would such a being, even if embodied as a Human Being, require a false, redundant self?"

Is an Ego even necessary? Why?

Perhaps because we've mistaken the Ego for the Self.

In our increasingly raucous culture, it's easy to lose touch with the higher truths. We stop thinking about Body, Mind and Spirit. Instead, we concentrate on the body, caring for its needs, acquiring things to protect, dress, promote and feature it. It wouldn't be much of a stretch to begin to identify with the body, and all the things required to make it the center of attention. Not long after that, we might also identify with "our" thoughts, ideas, perspectives, viewpoints, considerations, etc.

If we mistake the body for the being, then it's increasingly easy for us to mistake the ego for the self. And we begin a long downward and fruitless spiral: promoting an empty mask and protecting the shell; while forgetting who and what we really are... Then of course, it's easy to identify with all the fears, harsh memories and painful prior experiences which threaten the body and the ego... Soon, avoiding physical or mental pain, becomes our sole pastime. We are addicted to the substitute, fighting to preserve it, as we move further away from who and what we really are.

Anything that has to fight for survival is a physical entity.

Anything which wants to be preserved, is not the witness.

Anything which can be seen or heard, is not the witness. Not the self.

It is the self which does the seeing. The self is what and who we really are.

Nothing, If Not Critical*

"There, in retreat behind the endless battlements of my hidden standards, I am untouchable. Nothing is good enough, solid enough, strong enough, intelligent enough or well enough conceived to reach me. I am forever Safe from Engagement."
— Jennifer StJohn

Critic/Criticize/Criticism
(Noun) A person who expresses an unfavorable opinion of something. EG. "Critics of the new legislation say it is too broad."

Synonyms: condemning, reproving, disparaging, disapproving, scathing, negative, unfavorable, unsympathetic

I don't suffer fools lightly. Too many things, too many organizations, too many books, too many works of art, too many movies are not well built, not well designed, not well thought out, not well marketed, not honestly sold, not well intended. There's just so much stupidity, and laziness out there; forget the destruction, meanness and self dealing in the public sphere. It's difficult, if not impossible to find things,

> people or experiences that can stand up to a hard look. Life is pretty disappointing!

Success Reluctance is difficult to spot. In this case, it hides behind the language of criticism.

Do you have an intelligent, discerning friend who is perennially unimpressed? Someone who is just so smart and world weary, that nothing can clear the palisade of their superiority and the withering assault of their critical faculties?

Is it possible that such a person is (consciously or unconsciously, even sub-rationally) using their intelligence to keep the world at a distance — out of self defense?

Being critical is a commonly used "defense against life." It keeps things, experiences, ideas and people "at a distance" by finding them "un-acceptable in advance." If they don't satisfy the unexpressed expectations, the critical perspective, the hostile mindset, ideas, or experiences may be freely rejected without actual first-hand interaction.

Habitually critical people are, by definition; Success Reluctant. How can one succeed at anything in life without engagement? How can one grow without experiencing, interacting, "dancing" with what's new? Of course, one might suggest that an absence of a Critical Perspective would open the gates to everything and anything! "Without judgement, how can we protect quality, character and value?" True, True! But we are suggesting that it is redundant criticality, exercised unknowingly and habitually; that deserves examination.

Chronically critical people find themselves, over time, living within a steadily shrinking life perimeter, as everything new is consistently rejected. The realm of "what's acceptable" decreases, until "leaving the safety of home" itself becomes a "dangerous" option. The chronic critic becomes an "Excuse Factory" of ever so reasonable excuses for greater distance from life.

You can recognize Toxic Criticality by the fact that it pops up whenever something new presents itself. It forestalls connection, risk, entertainment, intimacy, originality, and; communication itself. It simply dis-connects the being — out of a mis-placed and mis-understood "self"-- defense. Ultimately it injures the very being it was conceived to protect, by cutting off access to everything required for a full life. Of course, this acidic "bad habit" continually reinforces itself, both in private sanctums, and in the safety of anonymous social media, where the sour bile of complaint and blame attract crowds with a penchant for tearing down what others have built.

Hidden in plain sight, Habitual Criticality is the dangerous obsession. It seems benign, protecting one from all manner of damage; but also, all manner of novelty and direct experience.

---

*With respect for the evanescent Robert Hughes, whose critical insights both entertained and educated his readers. His intelligence and insight raised the words "Art Critic" to a higher plane and personified rational criticism.

Crater in the Soul

"You think knowing [who your parents were] will heal you; fill some crater in your soul?"
—**Shen**, speaking to Po, the *Kung Fu Panda*
Kung Fu Panda II

My life is a story!

My family disowned me...

My church branded me and turned me out!

My friends found out about my private considerations and walked away...

My health has been tenuous and a constant challenge.

My work crisis has left me poor.

Man, I have had a difficult existence, and I'm suffering through tough times!

So how can/will Holosphy solve all of those realities?

Many people seem to suffer a "Crater in the Soul." They are endlessly seeking — something. But often they're just not too clear about exactly what is it they seek. It's a hunger, a desire, a need, a driven search for approval, for certification, for professional credibility — all of which must come from someone else, from something else, and from somewhere else. This "constant craving" for a fixing — always looking outward "over the next hill or back to that outrage in childhood" is a standard part of existence for many. Endlessly un-satisfied with themselves, with life, with everything.

There's the Professional Development Devotee — always on her way to the next seminar, the next training day, the next association membership. She's talented, articulate, smart but unfulfilled. She's got to get that next certificate.

"The Joiner," the young man who's a member of everything — yet still searching for approval, for stature, and deeply afraid of being revealed as a fraud.

What if the real issue with such people is not the missing validation from Mom or Dad, not from a university or a professional association — but instead, release from the self-created considerations of personal inadequacy?

What if the problem isn't what Dad never said, but about your considerations about his failure to validate? There's what he did or didn't do (probably a long time ago); and then there's how you reacted to that. And while all that happened a long way back — your own ancient responses are as real and as urgent as one second ago. And you are keeping them with you for constant reference and reflection. (Aren't you?)

Why keep them?

We suggest that happiness, satisfaction and self-worth originate from within, that we create our own happiness, our own sense of self-worth by examining our own existence, our own considerations, our own self-imposed programming, and discarding that which doesn't serve the best.

We suggest that the answer lies not out there, but in here! It lies not with them, but within you! Try removing the fixed consideration that things aren't; and can never be satisfactory.

Can this idea work…

1. In You?

What if every crater in the soul, was actually subject to resolution through introspection? We suggest that much of the pain of humanity is enhanced and amplified through layers of pre-existing considerations, old experiences, past solutions and intellectual explanations — all of which "cement the individual into their case." An alternative perspective, Holosophy suggests that through guided introspection and step-by-step examination, an individual can slowly deconstruct their own "downfall," then enhance, expand and improve their perspective — and hence their life.

2. In the Family?

We — all of us — have a tendency to draw "conclusions

about the future" based on imperfect readings of the past. What if the past needn't have such a bearing on the future? We suggest that you can positively influence your mate, your kids and your siblings and parents by encouraging them to slowly discard the burdensome considerations about life they've constructed and carried with them..

Maybe there are no craters in the Soul — but only in the conclusions we reached at the time.

Reluctant... to Stop

Success:
The Ability to Have. The Ability to Not to Have.
The Ability to Change at Will.

I'm not afraid of anything! I'm a huge success! I have a wildly successful career, a great family, a terrific impact on my chosen community, and I'm in demand from all quarters! I am the poster boy for Success! Even my mistresses are geniuses! I'm a leader and my opinions are sought after!

So what are you proposing to do for me? I have everything in the world I want, and a lot of things I don't want... or need. And I'm a little worried about never having enough. I'm concerned that someone might see through my carefully crafted exterior and discover the uncertain, self-critical guy inside. But this is the very definition of "Success!" Right?

Well, it's certainly a lot of everything, isn't it? Obviously the prevailing definition of success is to HAVE whatever you want, in whatever quantity, for as long as you choose. And, there are billions who wish they could experience your life…

We demur. Let's take a moment and acquaint you with "Nothing."

You know, that experience when you have no particular thought? No immediate need to initiate, respond, or react. No particular hunger, no immediate desire. No electronic demands for your time or attention…

No worries. No upsets. No demands. No emergency project requiring completion… No bill collectors. No sales calls to attend to. Just a comfortable empty space and time. Bliss!!!

For many "successful people" there's an overwhelming sense of "Too-Muchness." They've gotten so used to going, rushing, traveling, succeeding wildly, taking on more, going somewhere else. For these "Wildly Successful Alphas," the nature of "Success Reluctance" is in being "Reluctant, unwilling or unable to Stop."

So, it's not always about doing, or being or having MORE! It might also be about being, doing or having LESS!

The point is, *freedom* to choose, and then,
actually *choosing* - **to stop!**

Committed to Self-Destruction

"How did the rose ever open its heart
and give to the world all its beauty?
It felt the encouragement of light against its Being.
Otherwise we all remain too frightened."
—**Hafiz**

Look, I know you guys are well-intentioned.

I know you mean well.

But I've been on this path a long time, and I know down in the very seat of my existence that the only answer to my miserable life, is the endless and dedicated search for the achievement, recognition and love that my parents, my life, my circumstances and my creator have seen fit to deny me...

> I'm just not worthy. I know it. And I've never measured up to the standards that any truly deserving creature can manifest on their worst day... I just don't fit the bill, make the grade or qualify for the program.
>
> Just shoot me! Oh never mind, I'll do it myself... Or at least find a mate, boss, colleague or friend who I can enlist to hand out the criticism that will confirm my jaundiced self-image.

We know a woman, disgusted with herself. Beautiful, smart, well-traveled, loving and dedicated to helping — everyone but herself.

That's where the goodness stops!

She longs for companionship, then brings home a guy who is hostile, hard and given to days of silence. It seems, he's as dedicated to being mean as she is to being abused: the perfect couple! Did she really allow her inner doubts to choose her partner?

No sooner does she exit the scene in a teary moment of sanity — departing just before the abuse descends to physicality — then she returns to the repeated litany of self-abnegation. "I'm not good enough! I don't work hard enough! I can't do it! Who am I fooling? Nobody in their right mind would care about me. I can't learn anything!" Reciting this catechism of self-destruction can't be helping; but it does shore up the one thing she's certain of: She's no damned good!

Of course, the world is full of people who are down on

themselves; but few of those have this woman's incredible level of skill, good looks and sheer magnetism. Great ability, and a "Case" of equal magnitude!

A "Case" indeed. Was it Father, or Mother who convinced her that self-appreciation is unwise and inappropriate? Someone had a strong hand in instilling that programming — it takes a big commitment to keep someone this strong down!

So what's involved in reducing a capable, intelligent and attractive individual to a self-destruction machine?

We suggest that somewhere in early life was a hostile, destructive individual —maybe more than one. That they (parent, sibling, extended family or teacher) created a stressful and omnipresent environment of fear, denigration and submission which gave our heroine a steady, self-reinforcing series of negative suggestions. Which she now plays out in an endless, self-reinforcing cycle.

All it takes is one, a First! Then other similar experiences bump up against each other and eventually create a log jam of self-destruction.

But there is hope. She doesn't have to listen — even if the voices are in her head.

Instead, she can study and become familiar with how to notice self-defeating thoughts, subject them to a rational evaluation of their truth or usefulness, then discard them when appropriate and move on. It becomes a habit: Optimization! It takes time to develop and it goes better with an advisor who has seen it before. We call it

"Cognitive Optimization;" and it takes place in the form of a "Transformative Dialogue."

It's not easy. Many of those old ideas are so deeply rooted that we mistake them for the truth! But a dialogue with a trusted advisor can lay out the principles, set up a program and make progress a reality!

It may be high time to build a bigger box!

Tyranny of Perfection

"Lord, what fools these mortals be!"
—**William Shakespeare**

"There is a field beyond all notions of right and wrong.
Come, meet me there."
—**Rumi**

I'm just a little bit disappointed. I live a good life. I'm quiet, a little reserved even. I take care of my family, my work, my company, the community, my church.

But I have to admit, that I'm a little disappointed in the way things are turning out. Nobody seems to be looking out for me.

And, while we're about it, I'm not too sure I like what I'm seeing out there. People are pissy, self-absorbed, self-indulgent, stuck in their own internal dialogue about their own tiny

> little lives and caught up in the ups and downs of their microscopic mentalities. They are unhelpful, critical, mean, jealous, egotistical, greedy and, all at the same time, superior.
>
> It's looking more and more inviting to me to retire to my home and my private collection of entertainment, food and diversion — if not heading out to the woods to live as a hermit.

Every one of those ideals, those perfect exemplars, those people you respect and look up to — are human. They have smelly feet, indigestion, they leer at women (or men) occasionally, and they sometimes scheme about "making out on a deal." Maybe they just cut someone off in traffic…

They betray your expectations and your unspoken trust and respect.

And when you discover that, up close and ugly, it's hard. Because it brings into question whether the other things you see as exemplary about them are somehow nothing more than a dreamy mirage. "How can this be? How can my idol — a living incarnation of perfection — also be happy sitting home unshaven, eating nachos and watching detective shows?"

It's either/or. She's either perfect — beyond reproach in all things! Or she's just a self-dealing, critical upstart! A or B? Which is it? And you slowly, deliberately withdraw sword from scabbard and prepare for the ritual beheading.

Pause for a moment, and wrestle with actual adulthood. You cannot control anything beyond your own actions.

You may not actually control your own thoughts. You cannot control the actions or thinking of other people, the company, the town, the nation or the world. It will all continue spinning whatever you think of it. And those people — the ones you admire — and the ones you don't — will keep evolving on their own paths to their ultimate ends. Doesn't matter if you approve or disapprove. Doesn't matter what you hope for. They are all independent actors. They're beyond your control. But you can break free of the Sub-Rational tendency to "have an opinion about everything" and a critical one at that.

So much uncontrollable chaos going on all the time. It's hard to confront. It's enough to make you put your head down and focus one foot... in front... of the other. But still, as you slog forward, the magnetic, hypnotic attraction of a perfect ideal, is a beacon pulling you toward a higher, cleaner place.

And over time, you don't revere a person anymore, no individual could ever achieve what you hunger for. Now, you're searching for something better, higher, more perfect, more meaningful, more sustaining.

And you dedicate yourself to this loftier ideal — maybe it's the law, perhaps religion, maybe excellent health, surpassing a design you thought was perfect, or writing a better sonnet, a more beautiful song. Sure, an ideal is always better to admire than a gritty sweaty person. But be careful of "Death by Idealism."

It sneaks up on you, "Idealism." Gives "meaning" to your life — context. Good. And then, you start holding your idealism up as a standard of aspiration for yourself, and other people. So you don't idolize people any more — but before you noticed, you substituted your "Ideal." And mere people just don't measure up. You're such an adult now. You know people are fallible, imperfect. Can't be trusted. Leave you standing there waiting for them at the appointment they failed to make. You **get** them, but you haven't **forgiven** them. But instead, there's always that perfect idea.

And without really becoming aware of it, you'd taken a step away from getting wrapped up in imperfect people and gotten wrapped up in a perfect ideal — which rapidly becomes an un-approachable summit from which you can look down and find others lacking by comparison.

"Wow, those guys are **low**! Look at them down there... Deplorable really. So sad."

Or maybe you beat yourself up as well: "Gosh, it's halfway to February and I haven't yet finished the New Years cleaning. I'm disgusting. Just proves what a slacker I am."

Interesting. We crash and burn when we put other people on the pedestal, and they disappoint. So we mature and put an ideal up there — and use it to crush other people — and ourselves — as failing to rise to the impossible standard.

Death by idealism. Ok, we maybe haven't risen to an insane level of destruction, but isn't this the way it starts? By finding others, then ourselves, less than acceptable? Lacking some all-important quality?

Back to that step-by-step, head-down slog toward oblivion. There's a very dark cave at the end of this road. As more and more people, and more and more undertakings fail to meet the ultimate standard, the safe places decrease in number, the road narrows and there is no one with whom to connect. That's it. The abyss. Up against a wall of our own making.

The apparent choices? Head down and pay no attention, or head up and fail to "reach the un-reachable star." Does that appear to be a rational, (or creative) choice?

So is there an answer?

We suggest Introspection.

Where does that sense that nothing is ever acceptable originate? And as we discuss that thought and its origin, the foundation of your internal universe begins to shift. The beginnings of sanity.

Then, Acceptance — in the moment.

Our bodies are limited. Our minds are immense. And our spirits — well, together we create and connect with everything.

So what if we accept a certain natural, human limitation?

What if we revel in the immanent manifestation of random, (or unrecognizably creative) infinite potential?

Accept. Then, consider something: a small inclination toward a tiny incremental improvement. One small step, toward something a little better, like poking around in that sub-rational file for the moment when you adopted the crazy idea that perfect was ever possible.

That's it. The path to sanity in the chaotic world. No perfect heroes, no out-of-reach idols, no absolutes.

Just us, as we are, right here, right now. And a little bit better tomorrow…

Clinging to Case

"Nay, He stripped Himself of His glory, and took on Him the nature of a bondservant by becoming a man like other men."
—**Phillipians 2:7**, *Weymouth New Testament*

So I've been reading and having some new ideas about my life, and I've started talking to a few people about Self-development, Personal Responsibility, Cognitive Optimization.

But I'm finding that those conversations often die off as people begin to understand what all this implies... that one can really, definitely change one's circumstances (and maybe, ought to).

What's going on?

Why do people "cling to their case?" Perhaps because having problems, difficulties, scrapes, confusions, failed communications, financial difficulties and continuous volcanic upsets makes one (proves it, even) undeniably — human.

"If you hurt me, do I not bleed?" Being hurt, victimized even, is very convincing. It sort of proves that one is human — that is — not godlike.

Not above those strikingly human and ordinary problems. Therefore, not subject to loftier standards or expectations. Off the "divine hook" as it were... Convincingly and safely ordinary. Comfortably un-threatening.

Does an actor enjoy playing their part, relish it, even? If that's true, it might account for how careful people are about miraculously and spontaneously healing from hurt, illness or painful experience. Resurrection, as it were, "ends the play."

But from a Holosophy point of view, the issue isn't to throw off all bonds and limits of humanity, but to become more intimately aware of all bonds and limits — especially those that are redundant, unconscious and unnecessarily self-limiting. Then, clearing away the Sub-Rational fences and embracing genuine human limits.

Humanity is itself an acceptably and even beautifully circumscribed undertaking and life observes its own complex set of "divine boundaries."

But Sub-Rational and self-destructive fences and barriers are not required. As we become more aware of how we naturally function, we can also notice where and how we have added to our divine limitations by unconsciously and self-destructively assuming greater burdens than life itself requires.

The references to god(s) taking human form to enter the earthly sphere are too numerous to recount. Being human presents certain features: limitation of reach, form, duration and capability. "Birth" sets a clock ticking…

To a human, humanity may seem inexorable, painful perhaps, and normal.

But to a god, such an existence might seem desirable, even beautifully humble.

If such were the case, one would hardly rush to be relieved of that hard won, even chosen form of understated limitation.

To keep it in place, one might even resort to "claiming to be ordinary."

Presumably, though, any **redundant** burden may be laid aside without harm.

Cling to life, to humanity! But, lay aside the case!

Behind the Barricade

"Barricades of ideas are more powerful than barricades of stones."
—José Martí

Barricade: 1. A fortification, made in haste, of trees, earth, palisades, wagons, or anything that will obstruct the progress or attack of an enemy. It is usually an obstruction formed in streets to block an enemy's access. **2.** Any bar, obstruction, or means of defense. **3.** To fortify or close with barricades, to stop up, as a passage, to obstruct, as, "the workmen barricaded the streets of Paris."

> I discussed Holosophy and some of its core principles with friends over dinner. They reacted with an almost strategic retreat and defense, criticizing me, and my motives in bringing up this new idea of Cognitive Optimization.
>
> It was strange... They impugned my credibility

Holosophy - Conquering Your Fear of Success

> and that of "whatever quack made this stuff up." They began defending their supposed "Entitlement" to be outraged and upset by life, and subsequently defensive about the dubious benefits of self-development.
>
> It was almost as if they felt some kind of "positive connection" to their sense of "well-earned victimhood."
>
> I began from the assumption that people would be in a hurry to self-review and shed the self-imposed burdens of Sub-Rational memories and conclusions.
>
> What am I missing here? Is there some kind of "value" in victimhood?

Life behind the barricade is not posh, not civil, not comfortable. No water, no climate control, no shelter, minimal food, no sanitation. It's existence; but barely. Dug in and waiting for the anticipated attack that must come, or else "Why the desperate resistance?"

In the French Revolution, there actually were attacks by real enemies.

But today, many live their entire lives behind "Barricades of Ideas."

Many people exhibit an obdurate unwillingness to open the door to new ideas, an ongoing dedication to the status quo — even one in which they are apparently victimized.

What accounts for this? People are often happy to complain, but reluctant to change anything. Don't mistake the willingness to complain for the willingness to take action. They are almost happy and fulfilled in their complaints. Continual Upset is, in its own strange way, a "kind" of having. Changing would eliminate the victims' claim to compensation.

As loud as the complaints might be, people are often quite comfortable "behind the barricades," and completely unwilling to recognize them as self-erected. There can be a "rightness" to victimization.

If things don't change, perhaps it is because we are all (to differing degrees) present for and invested in the existing state of affairs.

Change requires recognizing that nothing happens exclusively **to** someone. It also happens **with** them. If you're not physically there, you can't be hurt. If you're not spiritually there, you can't be implicated. So if things are to change, you must stop being present for the outrage, and stop investing in the way things are, or were.

Before the shouts of outrage drown out the discussion, pause and consider: Who benefits? Obviously? Privately? Subtly? Irrationally? As you look at life more deeply, the differing and unique personal agendas begin to reveal themselves. Some benefit by employing impoverished garment workers. Some benefit by buying inexpensive clothing or cool electronics. Some benefit by leading the hue and cry about impoverished workers — not in their homeland, (the outrage business is not profitable there). Some benefit by earning only enough to appear impoverished. Some benefit by giving money to outraged cheerleaders and so, feeling morally superior. With so many benefitting, no wonder things continue.

If the workers refused the work. If the factory owners built somewhere else and paid greater wages. If the customers refused to buy from the owners. If the agencies refused the advertising revenue. The list goes on. The composite reality is a complex and interwoven equation of exchange/counter exchange across life's multiple dimensions. Victim-hood and outrage, are as old as time because perhaps, some of us see them as useful and even, valuable.

Isn't the idea of life to make progress — "to get up and out of here! To go higher and further!"

Well perhaps, but obviously not right away, and perhaps not in a single lifetime.

Betrayed

"Your trouble is, you've got high expectations.
Me, I've got low expectations...
So I never disappoint myself."
—Laurence Coriat

I'm just not confident that people are trustworthy.

It seems to me that everyone is out for their own benefit these days, and if they have to run over you to get where they're going, that's fine with them.

And let's not forget the institutions. Are we supposed to trust the Banks? What about the Church? How about the International Olympic Committee?

The Government? The United Nations?

And my spouse is not so on top of everything either. I have my hands full! Life is just one betrayal after another! I'm so disappointed.

> I'm thinking that staying home and watching movies is the best way to spend my time.

Sometimes we see something in another, something ineffable, desirable, enticing — Hope appears. We hope for the true religion, a perfect love, an enduring profession, the support of a community. We start down the road of connecting or affiliating. Things look good! Hope rises and grows. We mistake our Hopes for Reality.

But Hope is an independent thing, subject only to one's own creation (and imagination). Then there's anticipation. Then unrealistic expectations.

Reality on the other hand, is what we agree upon together. And if there's anything really difficult to come by in the real world, it's agreement.

But it's harder to be disappointed if we *only* work with what we've agreed upon.

But hope springs, and we pursue it, as it circles higher. Wanting love, desiring affection, seeking approval, dreaming of comradeship.

Lifted by the strength of our imagination, we find higher and higher perches where (we think) we might see forever. We... believe! Then. Comes. Reality.

And we are, once again, "Betrayed and Alone."

But betrayal is more difficult if we begin with *rational, shared, warranted* expectations.

Going Robot

Frank Sinatra & Lawrence Harvey
in John Frankenheimer's *The Manchurian Candidate*

It's Friday afternoon and you pick up the phone. The speaker identifies herself as Agent Wilder of the Internal Revenue Service. You notice a chill in the air as the agent explains that they have not received your most recent tax payment. You request her number so you can evaluate your records and verify that you have indeed discharged your duty.

The weekend is pretty much given over to working through the last two years of tax records, checks and bank statements. Monday you're on the phone early to Agent Wilder and finish the process by emailing a photo of your check.

Yes, you're a responsible citizen. But have you given any thought to how your jaw muscles tightened during the first phone call and how you did not relax (or do anything remotely normal) during the entire weekend?

The Phrase "Going Robot" defines the curious fact that some life circumstances force us into a robotic way of behaving, absent fun, interaction, pauses or a lifelike approximation of real humanity. Why is it that some circumstances, people and organizations freeze us into robotic compliance?

Some examples: the IRS, the Office (or schoolyard) Bully, the Bank, Law Enforcement, the Health Insurance Company, the Weather, Mom, the Coach.

We suggest that "Going Robot" is just another indicator that one has descended into the Sub-Rational and lost contact with their Rational, thoughtful self.

Poised for Outrage!

"Don't understand me so quickly!"
—**Yul Brynner** as **Chris**
in *The Magnificent Seven*

Have you noticed that people are "Poised for outrage"? Cutting you off halfway through a sentence? That they see you as "evil incarnate" before they've heard your entire premise? Especially when there's an emotional charge in the air? There are lots of reasons: high-pressure circumstances, high-speed technology and, of course, microwave popcorn.

Everything moves faster these days — faster than we can process. Knowing this, should we take more time to fully consider our response? Shouldn't it take longer to decide, than it takes to read the message? While we can connect quickly today, it still takes time to *fully comprehend the intention* of the sender. Comprehension requires actual consideration. I wonder if many of us are looking for confirmation of what we already believe, rather than a reasoned consideration of an issue.

There may be something deeper here and perhaps darker as well — the "magnetic desire for opposition." Remember the elementary school magnets and the "field effect" where the two opposite poles would line up and snap together? Is there a similar effect in human interactions? An individual makes a point, the field effect kicks in and people "click into opponency" while "understanding too quickly!"

Nice, neat, immediate and probably incorrect. Too many "instant polar opposites" out there? So many "soul of evil" opponents… We're skeptical of any conclusion arrived at in seconds, or even minutes. Yet all over the public sphere, people begin speaking, while others "understand them as enemies" — in nanoseconds. Apparently, the universe abounds with such "field effects." It's emotionally satisfying to be "Right!" while simultaneously making others "Wrong;" but this magnetic desire tends to overpower reason and thoughtful response.

We fail to take time to reflect and consider fully not just *what* people are saying, but *what they mean* by it, and what their underlying intentions are. If we "understand the other side too quickly," then allow the field effect to take over and place us into a neatly arranged opponency, we miss the chance to understand the depth of the other person's reason and character. If we act too quickly, we might miss someone who has something to teach, a unique viewpoint or a gift of truthful perception.

Of course, we can find ourselves in the opposite situation — "clicking into instant support" before a complete thought has been expressed. Many times our friends and colleagues are likely to "gloss over" the nuances in our position. While they are quick to express their commitment, they may not have grasped what they are being loyal to — and this unqualified, overwhelming support does a grave disservice to a true position.

Conclusions: Poised for Outrage? Poised for Agreement? Instantly jumping to conclusions that support our pre-existing beliefs. We deem that to be a pretty clear indication that people are *not thinking*, but reacting. That's a definitive indicator of Sub-Rationality.

Only time and consideration allow us to penetrate the depth of an argument. Black or White are easy to perceive and often fall victim to the field effect. Shades of grey and nuanced logic require a certain depth of discernment that only comes with time, patience and careful thought.

Applications

1. Individually

Resolve not to interrupt. "Listen the other person out." Allow the urge to react to pass before responding.

2. At Home

Notice that in close emotional quarters, the field effect is always poised to position the other in an all too easy and all too satisfying position of "selected, elected opponency." Don't buy it. "Listen your sister, mate or partner out" and then allow reason — and a loftier purpose — to work.

3. At Work

As a professional: recognize that a "perceived opponency or support" might be "artificial." Take time to allow reason to work and suggest ways that both parties can win. We think that in corporate life, "slower is often better."

Do everyone a service — hold out for the deep understanding. It's always more satisfying than outrage. The first step toward a more Rational perspective, even without the intervention of Holosophy, is to make a habit of taking time to think. Few of us carry guns anymore, and this is no longer a western, but "Don't understand me so quickly!" is still great advice.

Shadow

"Look for what you cannot see..."
— Jennifer StJohn

"You can only learn so much from a dead fish!"
—**Dr. Milton Love**, Chief Research Biologist,
Marine Science Institute, UC Santa Barbara

So, I'm confronted with a challenge here.

What is it that actually constitutes Life?

If it's not the body, or not in the body; what and where is it? The Monotheistic Religions have all talked about the Soul. But they talk about it like it's something you have, but can't locate and that isn't yours.

And, you can't see, taste, touch or control it. But they can. And they'll hold the door to heaven for you if you buy an indulgence.

> So that story seems crafted "for the benefit of the teller (or seller)."
>
> Where does Holosophy come down on the "Soul?"

That's the problem, isn't it? We have living things all around us — including human beings. Yet, we can't account for what causes or comprises life itself. We know it by its presence — or by its equally telling absence. But we can't account for the what, the why or the how of it. Nobody owns or controls it. When dealing with the individual, we call it — a Holon. Life simply is or it isn't! "There's only so much you can learn from a dead fish."

As Michelangelo studied corpses to inform his anatomical drawings, he found the structures of the tissues, bones and sinews; but he could not find *the spark*. And as we rapaciously dissect the cadaver of the washed-up Oarfish on Santa Catalina Island; we seek information of course, but **insight** into the distinctive life formula is in short supply.

When the light in the eye is gone, life is absent.

We suggest that **consciousness at large**: Holos, is "the immaterial force which animates." A weightless, timeless, invisible, spaceless, immeasurable, ineffable nothing, which manifests in and through all living somethings.

The problem: When it comes to Life, one can't see the thing, but only the shadow it casts.

Self! Righteous!

"The real and true Self can never be attacked
and therefore requires no defense."
—Nouk Sanchez

"If I knew it was crazy, I wouldn't be doing it!"
— Jennifer StJohn

The Hallmark of the Success Reluctant Moment, is the tense, self-monitored, assertion of rightness and correct behavior.

We believe we're doing the right thing, because our survival-oriented Sub-Rational realm is sending up behavior instructions that seem to have worked before. But right in the midst of a high-powered, leveraged moment, the individual loses concentration and momentarily "winks out" while saying something incomprehensible. The scene blows up or collapses as a dark memory overrides the present moment and the individual is then stuck, now trying to explain behavior that seemed to them right at the time, but which obviously wasn't seen as for-the-best by anyone else.

We are finely tuned, always calculating what we deem to be the optimum outcome. But when our Rational self is overwhelmed by a dark memory, we end up replaying that old moment, which is unfortunately wrong, in this moment.

Nothing is harder to explain than having unconsciously spliced behavior from some previous decade into this afternoon. But not having really noticed it, we do try and explain it. And we end up with a spouse, friend or colleague who gives us that look, and the more we explain, the worse it gets.

The only relief comes with a moment of true Self-Awareness: "Hey, I've been listening to myself, and I'm not making any sense. Do I make any sense to you?" Pause for confirmation.

"Did I do that?" Pause for confirmation. "I apologize! All right, I'm going to put myself on 'Pause!' until things settle down and I get myself together!"

A powerful clue, an indicator — that the internal thought process has gone off track, is when you find yourself reaching, digging or creating explanations to "make yourself right."

Desperately "reaching for rightness" is the ultimate indicator that you couldn't be more wrong.

Walled Inside

"If we are upbeat and positive, we have keys to all doors...The world is all gates, all opportunities, strings of tension waiting to be struck. Conversely, a low hopeless spirit puts out the eyes; skepticism is slow suicide. A philosophy which sees only the worst dispirits us; the sky shuts down before us. Whatever our circumstances, we always have the power to choose our attitude, and this can change everything."
—**Emerson**

Our family was moving that day, but I got sick and had to go to the hospital... There were those guys who came in and held me down when they came in to take blood. It was horrible. Four times a day. It went on for weeks! And when I got out and came "home;" it was a whole different place — unrecognizable.

Now... I really don't like hospitals. And I don't much like nurses, or linoleum floors, the smell of antiseptic, white uniforms, or people taking hold of my hands; or feet when I'm lying down. I hate needles, blood and medical offices. And

> then, I get pretty nervous around moving day. I don't like watching people take things down from shelves, pack them into boxes, put them in big trucks; or the challenge of moving from one place to another. I just like to stay in one place…. Keeping to myself.

Something happened! And we'd rather not experience anything even remotely like that, ever again! When, against all our attempts to avoid it, we do get into a situation that looks, smells, feels or resembles one of those earlier moments, we tend to drop right down into a Sub-Rational wavelength, lose a certain amount of conscious awareness, and try very hard to get somewhere else, fast!

Hey, it's not pretty, not reasonable, not Rational, but a very ancient form of fight or flight which drives us to avoid any risk of repeating something we once saw as "risky."

The Good News: It keeps us "safe."

The Bad News: It keeps us from growing or expanding. In an interesting way, "Safe" may not be deadly, but it certainly isn't leading us higher.

So, while the process plays out differently for each of us, the net effect is this: We remain "safe, walled inside the garden of our ignorance." No matter what our nation or culture, "the shock and menace of the new" is something we avoid whether it is new *thinking*, new *being* or new *having* — we avoid it with an instinctive dedication to the way things *were*. Safe from the new, comfortable with the old.

And it's not just the happenstance of circumstance; it's our very carefully reasoned rationalization for not going out, not staying late, not inviting intimacy, the unwillingness to move, and the unreasoning fear of the entire medical pharmaceutical community. We're not just distant from everything our Sub-Rational mode can come up with, we're also distrustful and suspicious of anything new.

New people, new languages, new business projects, new locations, new modes of thinking?

All carry risk and invoke the comfort of the envelope, unless we counter our fear, and push it!

Problem: Summary

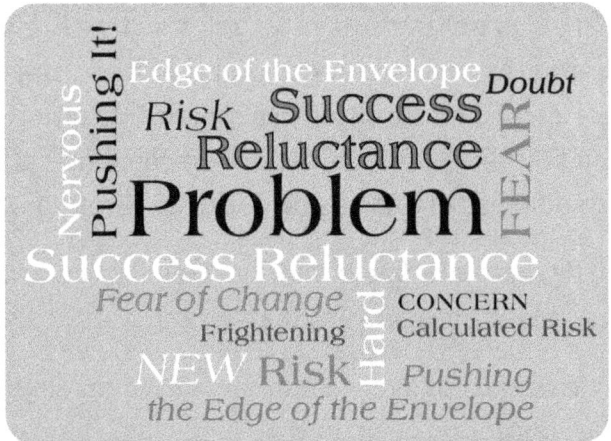

Success Reluctance does not equal or imply failure, but that the individual, while perhaps not failing, is not moving forward fast enough as desired. That middle ground of innocuous ordinariness is where so many unhappy lives, drab careers, empty relationships, and unconsummated marriages go to die, in the margins.

The symptoms of Success Reluctance can be found throughout the culture. People stop talking of important things. They gather less often. Companies stop innovating. Sales drop off. Tax receipts dwindle. Scholarships get smaller and fewer.

Educational institutions introduce fewer research projects. They focus instead on teaching social justice and comfort. Tenure is based on "going along and fitting in."

Government continues to intervene and "fix" outcomes with restrictive legislation and programs which benefit insiders and cronies.

People begin to value "the avoidance of failure" over "the potential for success."

Maybe it begins in infancy, elementary school or high school or in the endless exhortations to "Go to college! Get a degree and have something to fall back on if the arts career doesn't pan out."

A great many people, families, cities, states, and even nations are playing not to win, but to avoid or stave off a total loss.

Success Reluctance manifests in as many ways as there are people. Our cases are each unique in their manifestations, but alike in their causes — our own deeply instilled, reflexive defense mechanisms.

What we are talking about is our ever-present and automatic defense mechanisms which manifest every day in the form of what we find perfectly, repetitively comfortable, or terribly, reflexively uncomfortable; which create for each of us a series of unquestioned rules which we compulsively honor.

Avoiding an abject failure may be something less than the goal that sets a life on fire.

Section 3: Solution

What is Holosophy?

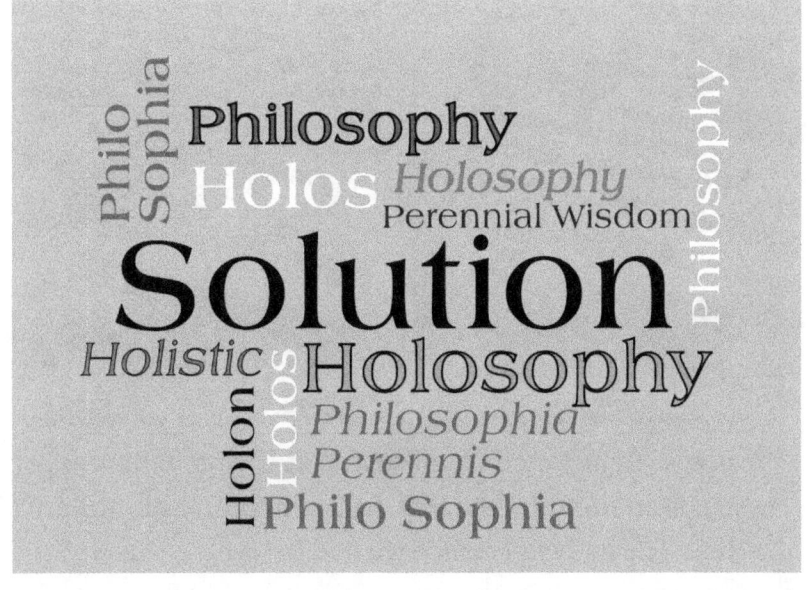

Solution: Overview

"You cannot solve a problem
with the same level of thinking
with which it was created."
—Albert Einstein

Success Reluctance, as discussed in the previous chapter, is an unremarked, but constant fixture of modern life. The bad experience we had before, sets us up to avoid repeating it in the future, but it also inclines us to avoid anything remotely (even indirectly) "connected or similar."

The individual's haphazard but systematic collection of such memories, fears, considerations and issues, constitute the Sub-Rational mind — an Envelope of Limitation. The sad truth is that any number of promising futures have been and are being short-circuited by our over-active, over-protective, automatic defense mechanisms. We're avoiding repeating past failure, but at the same time, forestalling future success.

Resolving the challenge of Success Reluctance requires more than simply noticing and becoming more aware of our avoidance tendencies.

A new level of thinking is required, which allows us to identify and systematically remove both the content and the mental circuitry which occludes our functioning. But accomplishing that objective has unexpected dividends. Exploring the mechanisms of Success Reluctance also reveals hitherto unnoticed aspects of the mind, body, spirit reality which can present the individual with a much wider, loftier life potential.

That new level of thinking, is Holosophy.
In this Section, we'll explore What it is, How it Works and the potential Benefits it can provide.

What If?

"Perhaps our ideas have us, rather than the other way around."
— Jennifer StJohn

Maybe it's never occurred to you, but…

What if:

Your "character" is not immutable?

Your circumstances are not fixed?

Your life story is not already written?

Your problems are not unresolvable?

Your wins and losses are not already decided?

What if:

You have choices?

You can influence what happens next?

You can decide how you feel about things?

You can influence the future?

You can bring about changes in your mood, your style, your level of intelligence, your income, your spiritual acuity, and your entire life?

What if:

That's been true all along?

It's really up to you?

You're actually in total control right now? (And have created this whole deal?)

Your own "mind" has been (and still is) your biggest enemy?

You can change everything by looking more closely in here, rather than out there?

What if… There's help?

What's Holosophy?

"Consciousness forgets itself for the sake of play...
It 'pretends to forget.'"
—**Amit Goswami**

Ok, so I want to be more...

I want to know how life works.

I want to feel more certain in my skin.

I want to connect better with life, people, living things, and creation.

I want the Great Wisdom. Is there such a thing...

I have found moments of insight in the martial arts, in artworks, museums, in the woods. But I think there's more...

I want to grow.

I want to feel comfortable at the table with big questions and big people.

I've seen a lot of things already, but most of them were not deep, significant or real.

I want more.

What is Holosophy?

Holos:

Whole, complete, unitary, self-contained, The Life Force.

Sophia:

Wisdom, the study of, knowing in the highest sense.

Holon:

The individual manifestation of a spirit player, the "being" in Human Being. Holos displaying as "one."

Holosophy:

An eclectic body of human potential thought, practice and education, devoted to improving and optimizing life and the ability to function.

Applied Philosophy:

Holosophy is designed to assist the individual in locating and removing cognitive barriers to growth, expansion and living life in full. This may include rehabilitation and re-establishment of an individual's control and enjoyment of their life circumstances; including enhanced and extended awareness and influence.

Holosophy is, in the simplest sense, high-wisdom codified... a body of philosophical Perspectives, Practices, Coaching and Counseling designed to optimize individual cognitive ability with the goal of assisting the individual in re-establishing their awareness of and connection to the source of Life itself.

Holosophy exists to assist individuals in optimizing their

cognitive abilities and personal insights, and through Transformative Dialogue, to notice and remove any instances of Success Reluctance, barriers to expansion or self-imposed limitations.

What's a Holon?

Holon: Definition

The individual manifestation of a spirit player, the "being" in Human Being. "Holos" displaying as "one." One component (perhaps the most important) of a "Human Being."

In our view, a Human Being is a "composite" of Body, Mind and Spirit.

"Spirit," "Soul," and "Living Essence," all have a resonance, and relevance to this discussion; but all older names and words tend to carry some "intellectual freight," a holdover from earlier centuries.

Perhaps a new, "un-freighted" label is in order…"Holon."

The source of individual life. The spiritual component of

an individual human being. A Holon is without form, shape, charge or mass.

No location, no measurable energy signature.

A Holon possesses and uses a human body.

A Holon can perceive, calculate, form postulates and considerations, and can intend to create effects on the surrounding world through the brain and the body.

A body <u>without</u> a Holon is an empty shell.

A body <u>with</u> a Holon aboard is deemed to be fully alive.

Breaking Free

"Every next level of your life will demand a different you."
—Leonardo DiCaprio

The Problem:

Redundant, post traumatic memories, filed away, beneath the level of consciousness, until triggered and brought forward into the present by a moment of "similarity" to the earlier moment of formation.

This instinctual process, so useful in "fight or flight" emergencies, is both dangerous and debilitating at this point in our evolution.

More common than previously understood, such "flashbacks" can be triggered by anything, depending on the earlier, parent association.

The Solution:

Holosophy is dedicated to increasing awareness of the challenge posed by Success Reluctance. Engaging in Transformative Dialogue, the individual can discover and investigate the syndrome and steadily, gradually improve their understanding and mastery of their cognitive environment: a process we call Cognitive Optimization, or bluntly, "Thinking Better."

Changing Minds

The Guru's Cat
Each time the guru sat for worship with his students,
the ashram cat would come in and distract them,
so he directed them to tie it when the ashram was at prayer.

After the guru died, the cat continued to be tied at worship time.
And when the cat expired, another cat was brought into the ashram to make
sure that the guru's orders were faithfully observed at worship time.

Centuries passed and learned treatises were written by the guru's
scholarly disciples on the liturgical significance of tying up a cat
while worship is performed.
—**Anthony de Mello,** *Song of the Bird*

I don't want to change my world view.

I don't want to change my politics.

I don't want to change my ideas about the

Holosophy - Conquering Your Fear of Success

> "deep stuff." I don't actually want to go there.
>
> I don't want to change my ideas about my family. I've finally reached a state of resignation about them.
>
> I don't want to talk about my self-image. I like where I'm at!
>
> And don't come at me with some touchy-feely, new-age jargon!
>
> And while we're at it, no religion stuff, either! That's too spiritual for me.
>
> So. What do you propose to do for me?

Many have a deep and abiding commitment to their opinions, conclusions, suppositions, faiths and practices which were handed down through parents, schools, communities and churches, or in reaction to them. To these people, the option of "changing one's mind" may appear to be a violation of their integrity as a being.

But what if one's most significant ability is to be fully present, aware and interested at all times — willing to re-assess one's opinions, likes, dislikes, political stances, loyalties and ideas about politics, money, sex, work and religion? What if things change? Can you? Do you still harbor that commitment to Santa Claus or the Easter Bunny?

We're not suggesting that perspectives should shift with the tide. But what if, as circumstances change, new facts reveal themselves and as you mature; you find that it's time to re-assess (and maybe alter) your perspective, and your reality. It's simple really, when you realize the difference between continuity and stasis. (There is a difference, right?)

What we've noticed is that many people have a variety of ideas, thoughts, opinions and common "practices that have become stuck" — and in a funny way have begun to push back and influence all other mental activities.

Sometimes, it's as if these people have come *under the influence* of their thoughts, ideas, practices and opinions. As if some or all of those were actually "in charge." And from our perspective, that's a very dangerous place to be. After all, if your "mind" is in charge, who's in charge of it?

What if you are not your mind? Not your opinions? Not what your father taught you? What if you are senior to it? Many people feel that if they change their mind, they are also changing their deeply valued personhood... almost as if they *are* "their mind." To such a person, a change of mind, would be akin to death.

But then, you have changed your mind over time, haven't you? And you're still with us?

That's where the process begins.

If you can change your mind, you must be senior to it; and the one in charge.

We humbly suggest that "The Changer is Senior to the Change."

If you can see yourself thinking; are you the thoughts, the

brain harboring the thought, or the being — the spirit — the Holon, which uses the body, the mind and the brain?

If you are indeed that being; changing your mind may not be the end of life.

(It might be a beginning.) It might just be reality evolving.

Holosophy presents endless opportunities to re-set, re-define, re-evaluate and re-think your approach to, and considerations about, life. You may wish to free the Guru's cat. But you'll have to be able to change that mind.

Best Answer

"To be a good scientist, you have to use your heart
because that's where the information comes first."
—**Nassim Haramein**

"The basic rule of science: 'Follow the evidence, wherever it leads!'
But this can be a difficult rule to follow.
It is easy to spot the unexamined assumptions of others,
but harder to root out your own."
—**Anon**

"Watson, you will not apply my precept," he said, shaking his head.
"How often have I said to you that when you have
eliminated the impossible, whatever remains,
however improbable, must be the truth?"
—**Sherlock Holmes**

My relatives, their priests, my college professors, my coaches, and I agree: There is one true answer to every question.

All "others" are false.

> So as I consider this "new thing" in the human potential arena, I'm a little worried about having my pre-existing set of answers upended or discarded wholesale.
>
> My answers are important to me. Sort of like the scaffold around which I've built my life. Scaffold, armature, skeleton, internal structure... all of those words seem very similar in my mind to assumptions, beliefs, considerations, truths and commitments.
>
> I want to grow, but I don't want to accept or create a whole new set of doctrines, laws and rules!

Holosophy doesn't promise **The Answer**. Instead, we follow the time-honored tradition of continuing the endless search for **the best available answer at this moment in time**.

Obviously, in this field, we are dealing with issues, forces and realities that defy both science and logic. Yet it is clear that we are **not merely physical** or **intellectual creatures**.

Love, intuition, creativity, humor and commitment are not physical things. In point of fact, they are not "things" at all. But their existence demonstrates the multiple layers of life experience of which we can avail ourselves.

In our experience, the "What is Life?" question yields to the consideration that "Life is a Composite." There is a **Physical** aspect to life, an **Intellectual** aspect and a **Spiritual** aspect. There are "**Physical** Things," of course, houses and bigger buildings, automobiles, clothing, wine, food, beautiful accoutrements and money. Then there are the "**Intellectual** Things"; the great learnings, the knowledge that feeds the human aspiration for more, better, greater. And then, there are the "**Spiritual** Things," entirely non-physical aspects of our existence that make the physical things worth having: Love, Respect, Commitment, Family, Honor, Integrity, Humor... and perhaps, Irony.

So while the world seems constantly dedicated to finding answers, or **the answer**, we suggest a more nuanced approach; simply this: What's the **best** answer to the "What is a Human Being?" question? (Given the available information and tools...)

To begin, a simple hypothesis...

A Human Being, like life itself, is a composite:

A Physical Component — The Body/Brain.

A Mental Component — the Mind.

And finally, a Spiritual Component — the Holon.

We know this by simple experience. While we cannot offer "scientific" proof of the spiritual component of our lives, we can humbly point out that each of us has personally experienced the "loss" of a loved one. That moment when the life force departs constitutes "Evidence of Absence." Life itself, though ephemeral, is "evidently present." We recognize it by its presence; and by its absence. The tissue in the brain is not the character of the individual who uses it. The bones of the body are not the character of the individual who uses them. But the being (with a character) who *inhabits* a body and *commands* physical existence through the mind/brain is what animates human existence.

However improbable, that's our best explanation. It defies science and reason, but fortunately there's more to life than those powerful, yet limited, tools.

We suggest that the "Best Answer" approach can suffice for practical purposes, until a more complete and "scientifically acceptable" rationale presents itself.

Further, if we suppose this perspective to be valid and test it against our life experience, perhaps our day-to-day practical experiments will yield a "hands-on" reality against which to test our suppositions/hypotheses.

While we have profound respect for Occam's Razor as a rational asset, we also keep both Shakespeare and Antoine de Saint-Exupery in mind.

"There are more things in heaven and earth,
than are dreamed of in your philosophy, Horatio!"
William Shakespeare
Hamlet

"One sees clearly only with the heart.
Anything essential is invisible to the eyes."
Antoine de Saint-Exupéry
The Little Prince

Brain *Receives* Mind

"There's a fundamental field of information that is the source of our consciousness. Consciousness is not an epiphenomenon of your brain. It is actually something that your brain is "tuned-in to" like a radio is tuned to a frequency."
—**Nassim Haramein**

"Peace is the natural state. The mind obstructs that innate peace. There is no entity by the name: Mind. Investigate the mind and it will disappear. Because of the emergence of thoughts, we surmise something from which they start... That we term Mind. That place from which thoughts originate, we term Mind. When we probe to see what it is, there is nothing like it. It disappears. After it has vanished, peace will be found to remain eternal."
—**Sri Ramanah Maharshi**

"My brain is only a receiver. In the Universe there is a core from which we obtain knowledge, strength, inspiration. I have not penetrated into the secrets of this core, but I know it exists."
—**Nikola Tesla**

"The brain may exist in order to prevent thought."
—**Robert Thomas**

"The brain acts as a 'reducing valve.'"
—**Aldous Huxley**

Which am I?

Where does that stuff happen? You know, "Thinking?"

Does it take place in the left big toe? Perhaps the right ear lobe? No? Not the digits? Wait, I sometimes "get" feelings that seem to originate in other body parts (GUT Reactions.).

Maybe that stuff happens in the head, wait, not in the head, not in the brow ridges, not the hair, not the brain stem exactly — aha the Brain! But no, because there is so much going on under the heading of "MIND and MENTAL" and these are not merely biological or mechanical or computational occurrences. Thinking, calculating, organizing, composing, feeling (emotions vs. pain).

Does all this go on in the head, in the brain? As it moves from horizontal to vertical, from the bedroom to the board room? Really? All of it? That's what "I" am? A particular brain? Wet, bloody, fluid-encased grey matter? Located in a particular body part? Or part of a part?

Am I that "thinking?" That "thought? Or this one?" That "Idea?" That "Memory?" If not that "one," then am "I" the entire body? The entire brain? Stem and all? Am I "All Those Thoughts?" What happens when "I" cannot think clearly?

Am I those voices in the mind? Or am I the witness to the voices? Or am I the feelings which seem to emanate concurrently with the voices?

Clearly, I have to do some "thinking" about what "I" actually "am" and what exactly constitutes and distinguishes "me" from others, and "me" from "it" (this body/brain/mind/thoughts/feelings).

Here's an idea: Brain tissue is "receptive to thought." But — like a Wi-Fi network, serves to receive and re-broadcast content — not always discriminating about *which* thought or *whose* thought is received.

While you may enjoy a certain "primacy by occupation" where your body is concerned, any errant mind, broadcasting in the neighborhood may be picked up and re-broadcast as well.

Consider the brain/body system as a "receiver of content." What's being received, however, doesn't originate in the tissues, nor in the receiver.

The "Mind" (and all "minds") are *outside* the brain *and* the body. So, don't mistake *yourself* for *those thoughts. (And don't mistake any or all of those thoughts for you!)*

Many of our challenges arise because a thought passes in front of our eyes and we just reflexively "own it" and act on it. Sometimes a crazy, mean, obnoxious thought passes in front of our consciousness and we decide (maybe mistakenly) that it's ours. Then we're embarrassed, maybe ashamed, then we try to erase it or shout it down.

But, what if thoughts just… come? And what if they… go, just as easily?

What if the mind is a tool that we can use or ignore, or fine tune, to employ as a tool to help us gather information, to synthesize new ideas, to formulate a point of view or a strategy, or to write a story or presentation?

Maybe this tool can be "optimized" to be more useful, and

less subject to distraction.

This isn't mind control or hypnosis, but an exercise in discrimination.

We call it "Cognitive Optimization" (Improved Thinking).

Is there a thought? Is it coming from a place or an event that may have a lesson for you? Is it yours? Is it helping? Do you choose to focus on something else?

That's it. It takes a while to develop *skill* at the process of discrimination, and a certainty that you can do it independently at any time.

Thoughts (and thinking) are tools, to be used, saved or discarded — at will.

Ultimately, the objective of Cognitive Optimization is to put you, once again, in control of thoughts. Create them. Expand them. Bring them closer, examine them closely and erase them. Explore them. Add to them. Build on them. Share them. Respond to them, rather than reacting.

Thoughts are "things" in the sense that they generate very small but detectable mass and resistance in the body as they come, go or pass, but they are not the same as "property" which can be obtained or disposed of in the physical sense.

We suggest, that this question is not subject to being solved by science, for science requires hypotheses, experiments and duplicatable results which deliver hard facts, and **the facts** are not yet fully in evidence. (But for the evidence that there is a weighty Grey organ, resident in the skull, which seems to have something to do with waking, consciousness and thoughts.)

A modest hypothesis:

You are "Not the Mind." This thing that you might lose, or be burdened by. Instead, It, in all its manifestations *is yours*, to serve as a receiver of information, and a doorway to consciousness. Beginning to see it dispassionately, as something which can be controlled, and something that serves your needs and interests…

Well, that would be a good start!

Out of Our Minds

"Our memories are card indexes, consulted, then returned in disorder by authorities whom we do not know and cannot control."
—Cyril Connolly

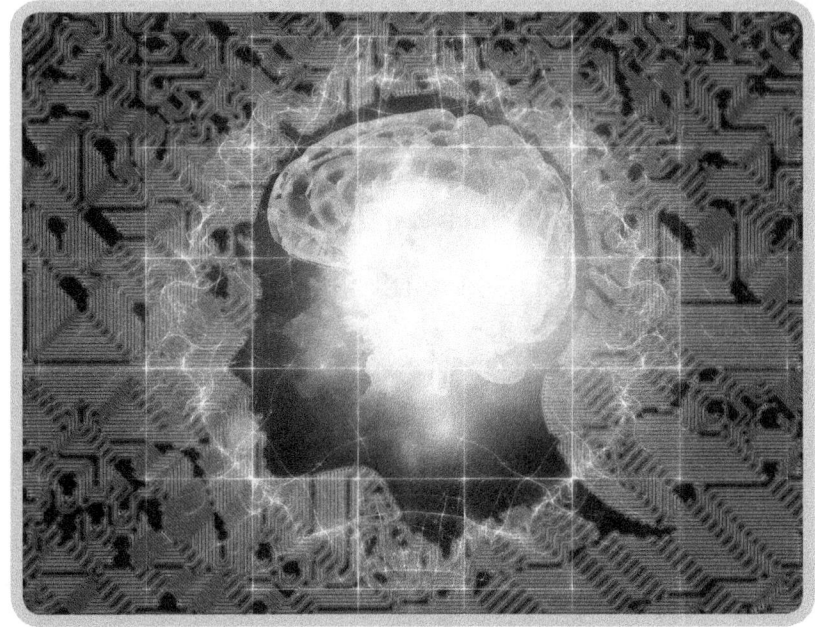

Why are we crazy some times, about some things, and around some people, but only in some circumstances?

How is it that we can build such masterpieces of physical engineering, and yet be unable to de-bug the internal engineering of our own minds? Why can't we see through our own viewpoints and become more objective about solving our own internal problems?

We suggest that the problem lies in our engineering, and our outside-in, medically centered approach to helping ourselves.

Recent History of Mind

The love and study of thinking have always been subject to lively debate. The Perennial Philosophy continues to evolve as we speak. Some signal contributors:

Freud suggested that certain kinds of previous events leave traces in the mind, which are able to exert influence on current thought.

Jung postulated a "Collective Unconscious," which complemented Freud's discussions about Id, Ego and Super Ego.

Reich moved the discussion forward with the concept of "Character Armor," the burdensome ancient defenses carried forward.

Hubbard moved the theorizing forward still more with the notion of a Reactive Mind, a stimulus/response repository of Engrams. Holosophy, we suggest, builds upon these foundations.

Where and What is Mind? How does it differ from Brain?

We don't know precisely Where the Mind is, What the Mind is. It is difficult to explain thinking, remembering, feeling, perceiving or considering... You know, "the stuff" "the mind" "actually does."

With no physical place, no physical space, we're prepared to consider that obsessing about location or physical composition may be a fool's errand, because we are discussing "things" that are not "things" in "places" which are not really "places."

(See: Brain Receives Mind, page 135.)

But, though hard to locate or completely explain, activities of mind are, to a significant extent, "describable."

3 Kinds of Mind

"There's a lot going on. Lots of calculating, "mental" activity, layers of frequency. Above Consciousness: there is connection, inspiration, higher awareness. There is Consciousness: logic, response, calculation, evaluation of options. Beneath Consciousness: there is instinct, reaction, self-preservation, algorithm."
— Jennifer StJohn

The wonder we describe as "Mind" is indeed, many things operating across a dynamic and fluid range of "frequencies" which are devilishly hard to quantify. Still, we can describe their disparate qualities with such specificity, that we can agree that thought, reaction, perception, emotion, connection and reason are similar enough, person to person, that we, appear to "have them in common." We suggest three broad categories:

Sub-Rational Mind
(Pavlovian, Dark, Reactive, Harsh History, Judgmental, Robotic, Fearful)

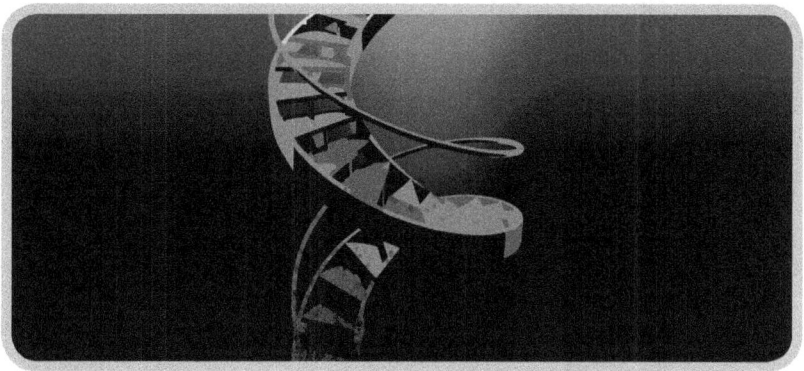

A redundant storehouse of memories acquired and retained under stress, preserving and protecting the "Self" of that moment and the singular values, definitions and perspectives acquired and contained within it. Survival focused, reflexive, reactionary, programmed, occluded, opinionated, spuriously certain, hyper-emotional, conditioned response, sometimes destructive and judgmental. Also highly critical and oriented to "creating victim-hood" or high-powered "villany." When accessed under similar stress or trauma, produces overpowering reactions to stimulus and short-circuits rational consideration. Behavior extending from sub-rational stimulus is unquestioned and viewed as "right and proper." It is, after all, one's own information and experience being brought forward, but now with an overpowering overtone of stress-formed emphasis.

We are, apparently, designed to remember, perhaps even everything we encounter. But some memories (painful, life-threatening, survival-tinged, traumatic) are heavier, more magnetic, more charged with painful, emotional electricity. Hence, they seem to be redundantly stored, both as regular memories, but also grouped together in a special collection of threat-specific information which is poised to be called up in moments of stress or pain in order to contribute to self-preservation. This Sub-Rational Frequency is not thoughtful, not self-aware, not reflective, but poised to take immediate command and control of the being for "self-preservation in emergencies."

Rational Mind
(Responsive, Logical, Analytical, tends toward Either/Or - Plus/Minus)

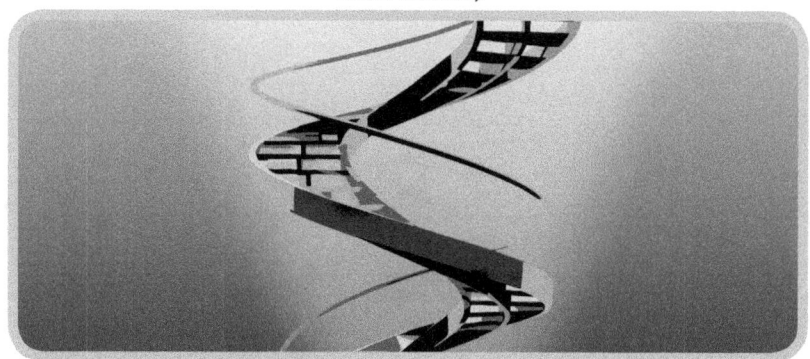

Analytical thinking through Binary Logic (Either/Or choices). Perceives existence from and through a single viewpoint. (Inclined toward a mono-dimensional perspective: Me/Mine/Self.) Able to Perceive, Intend, Interact, and Respond to stimulus in considered, thoughtful fashion.

The Rational or Responsive mode allows the individual to reason and respond to daily life, and reflects a functional, logical, safe, goal-oriented style of thinking, which might be labeled, "Business as Usual." Constructive, Transactional, Exchanging, Calculating, Factual Observation.

Supra-Rational Mind
(Communion, Imagination, Connection, Creativity,
Pre-Consciousness, Expansion, Intuition)

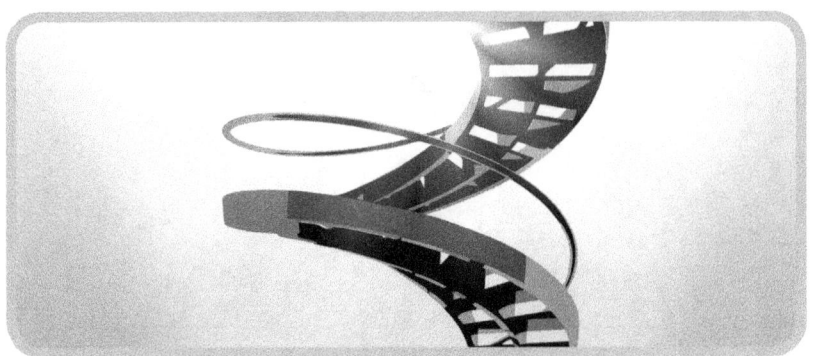

Guided by the Compass of Multi-Dimensional Ethics, and the Truth Functions, the Supra-Rational Mind can Perceive and Evaluate from multiple viewpoints and expand upon them or create entirely new, higher-level initiatives, projects and aesthetics at will. The Supra-Rational mode also opens to intuition, leaps of insight, and levels of creativity that may simply appear to be "Genius" when perceived from the other realms.

Cognitive Optimization

"Hawk: 'How'd you get me back?'
Black Widow: 'Cognitive Recalibration!'
I hit you really hard on the head!"
—*The Avengers*

There seem to be a lot of people and organizations with some kind of interest in my thoughts. People who want money. Organizations who want my eternal loyalty — and a percentage of my lifetime earnings... Clubs who want my credit card number. Card companies who seem to want to tell me where, when and how to travel. The local "Worship Center" promotes the "Gospel of Prosperity." Social

Media now seems to know and keep an archive of all knowledge, and they are constantly putting things in front of me in which, frankly, I didn't know I had an interest...

So, Optimizing one's Cognitive Abilities sounds good... But, does it involve hypnosis, trance, physical intimacy, a blow to the head, jumping in the river, a share of my estate, or ...

Hymns? No thanks.

Let me put this more clearly:

I don't want to "worship" something or someone...

I don't want to be told what or how to think...

I don't want to be told with whom I may associate...

I will read, study, discuss and eventually form my own ideas about the nature of the universe, divinity, creation, and my place in all of it...

But I would sure like some more undemanding, thoughtful discussion about all that.

As we categorize the ranges of mental activity, it becomes obvious that many of us, both at an individual and a cultural level, wrestle with descending into Sub-Rationality on a regular basis. One might even go so far as to consider that through war, disease and starvation, portions of the planetary community seem to dwell at that level, lost in an endless, repeating nightmare — re-experiencing the fall of civilization over and over again. Individually, however, we can often catch ourselves sinking into sub-rationality as our emotions, reactions and criticisms weigh us down, and keep a rational response out of reach.

Our objective with this categorization of mental activity by separate frequencies and realms is to clear a path for our own evolution, to dismantle the ascendancy of the Sub-Rational and find our way, first to a more broadly Rational and thoughtful state, to thrive in a world of shared reason.

Or perhaps, there's yet more, a life more often characterized by creativity, communion and connection — the Supra-Rational.

There is hope. Holosophy and its primary tools, Cognitive Optimization, and its means of implementation, the Transformative Dialogue, were founded with two objectives:

- To help humanity become aware that in spite of its knee-jerk nature, Sub-Rationality can be overcome.

- To provide a practical path out of the Sub-Rational realm, into and through the Rational, to ultimately ascend, both as individuals and as humankind, into a more regular abode in the Supra-Rational.

Cognitive Optimization is the ongoing process of

increasing self-awareness and choice about what one values; and to what degree one desires to increase their own ability to perceive more accurately and perform in a more optimum way.

Getting from "Here to There" is the ultimate personal journey. Through counseling, Sub-Rational structures, memories and their influences are progressively removed; allowing the individual to move toward more Rational and finally Supra-Rational/creative modes of awareness, thinking and behavior.

The Goal:

Restoration of a more complete, enlightened and able player, with continuous, gradually expanding awareness and participation in all dimensions of existence.

The Process:

Holosophy, through the process of Cognitive Optimization and personal application in the Transformative Dialogues, provides a framework for directed individual intention; and a program of disciplined study necessary for graduated reduction and erasure of Sub-Rational life influences.

We deem this to be a great undertaking: to assist people as they change their minds, and then their lives for the better, not only for themselves, but for the benefit of everyone and everything they touch. Because each individual has a vast contact and connection potential across the Kosmos,* we know that improving a single individual (let alone many) can create unlimited positive results.

* **Kosmos:** an ancient Greek term used by Pythagoras to refer to the entire universe in all of its multi-dimensionality, i.e. spiritual, mental, emotional and physical...as contrasted with "Cosmos" in its modern usage which refers only to the physical realm.

Experience? or Engram?

"To Be or, Not to Be?" That is the question!
Whether it is nobler in the mind
to suffer the slings and arrows of outrageous fortune
or to take arms against a sea of troubles and, by opposing, end them."
—**Hamlet,** William Shakespeare

So I've been reading about traumatic stress injuries and the word engram came up. So, what's the difference between "Experience" and "Engram?"

They both arise from simple life experiences, don't they? Can something be a mere experience for one person; and actually be an Engram for someone else? And how can I tell?

Holosophy - Conquering Your Fear of Success

That is the question, isn't it? Is it just a bad experience? Or is it something larger and more dangerous?

If it's a bad experience, you handle it. You take arms... and end it! You get over it. You heal. You move on. You learn from the experience and take action to prevent its recurrence.

If it's traumatic, though, you flinch a little. It "affects" you. Perhaps it "owns" you! You suffer its slings and arrows. You stop seeing beyond it and get lost in the moment, recording and compulsively recreating the sensation, emotion, quality of the experience, the sound, the taste, the smell, the temperature, the touch, the background noises, the personalities, the emotional context — and you keep on doing that, and adding to the universe of Sub-Rational adhesions connected to the event — which keep on drawing in and accruing "Sub-Rationally similar" content from that moment on. All in the Sub-Rational attempt to warn you off and away from anything remotely similar in the future.

That's the difference.

The engram never leaves you, and it super-imposes itself on top of the underlying memory and puts an ever growing amount of emotional charge onto that experience and anything remotely similar for the remainder of your days.

For you, an experience might be new and not deadly serious! For me, however, this single event caves me in entirely! Because unknown to you, I had a similar event two years ago that left me injured. And worse, five years earlier, my mother died in a remarkably similar incident.

Each "related" event enlarged the case.

For one, it's an upset, an inconvenience.

For another, it's life-threatening, maybe crippling.

And, such events are cumulative: each one adds to the long list of related issues and items, which tend to magnetize more and more related content from each and every big and small event going forward — leaving you with a larger and larger case; and less and less energy and attention to handle day-to-day life.

A Case: A "Sea of Troubles" indeed.

The real difference? A traumatic event is "convincing." Instead of merely experiencing it and remaining at cause over your life and universe, you experience it more intensely — believing that you can be hurt, damaged, affected.

It's "Outrageous Fortune" that stays with you... in the form of the Sub-Rational.

The Transformative Dialogue

A good counselor listens for, and ultimately discovers what hasn't been said.

I've done some analysis. The endless rounds of "How'd that make you feel?" Drive me crazy. I'm not looking for reassurance, or for an endless parade of emotional responses. What I'm curious about is:

"Why I have such a hard time with women?"

"Why I can't face Public Speaking?"

"Why Older Men make me so crazy?"

"Why I get nervous when I have to talk about money?"

"Why those public gatherings to talk about politics make my heart flutter?"

"Why going outdoors makes me nervous and

> scared - especially at night?"
>
> "Why driving in the city is fine; but driving a coastal road terrifies me?!"
>
> It's not that I want to be validated in my crazy feelings or emotions.
>
> It's that I want to make those crazy moments and thoughts go away, without drugs or surgery!

Holosophy's most basic tool is the Transformative Dialogue. A conversation between two people; one who mostly talks (the Client), and one who mostly listens (the Counselor). There's a rough format for such conversations, covering the lead-up to the day's focus, then a review of the process, and a focus on a particular area of intense weight, or concern.

The Counselor's task is to provide an objective connection or base, to allow the Client to range back to an area of past traumatic stress, and to relate that material out loud in a way that allows it to be reviewed clearly in the present moment.

At the end of an incident, the Counselor can direct the Client to view that material from present moment perspective — which often results in a moment of intense new awareness. In the light of this new perspective, the material in question fades, vanishes and re-files itself as just another memory of a past event, but now without the weight of Sub-Rational survival importance.

The Transformative Dialogue requires no hypnosis, no trance, no drugs, no submission. It is simply a private conversation between one who looks, and one who listens, with the occasional coaching to go further, look deeper, or repeat the process in search of additional information.

There are several aspects of the Dialogue which provide significant relief:

Returning Directly to Traumatic Moment.

Gently but repetitively reviewing all the included material until the importance attached to it slowly, but permanently fades.

The challenge of other rehab and relief techniques is that they attempt to resolve post-traumatic issues by talking about them, without ever directly looking at them.

In our experience, when you look at something directly, it tends to evolve, come into focus, then slowly vanish.

Counsel/Tutorial

Acquiring Knowledge is primary.
Applying Knowledge is critical.

Holosophy is a combination of two important components: The Acquisition of Knowledge, which we call Tutorial; and the Application of Knowledge, which we call Counsel.

Both are fundamental undertakings.

Tutorial: Adds information, practical tools, teaches and exercises the basic skills. It also gives the newer client and practitioner valuable exposure to experienced advice.

Counsel: Applying the new knowledge and skills in the context of the Transformational Dialogue; the place where the art is practiced... erasing Sub-Rational content.

(If it can be erased, it's Sub-Rational.)

Tutorial/Counsel Commentary

In many cases, someone begins acquiring information as a client, applies it to their own benefit and decides to become a counselor to others; in which case, the information acquired from their own tutorial gives them a leg up on the development of their counseling skills.

Erasure

"To cease creating is the basis of erasure."
—Robert Thomas

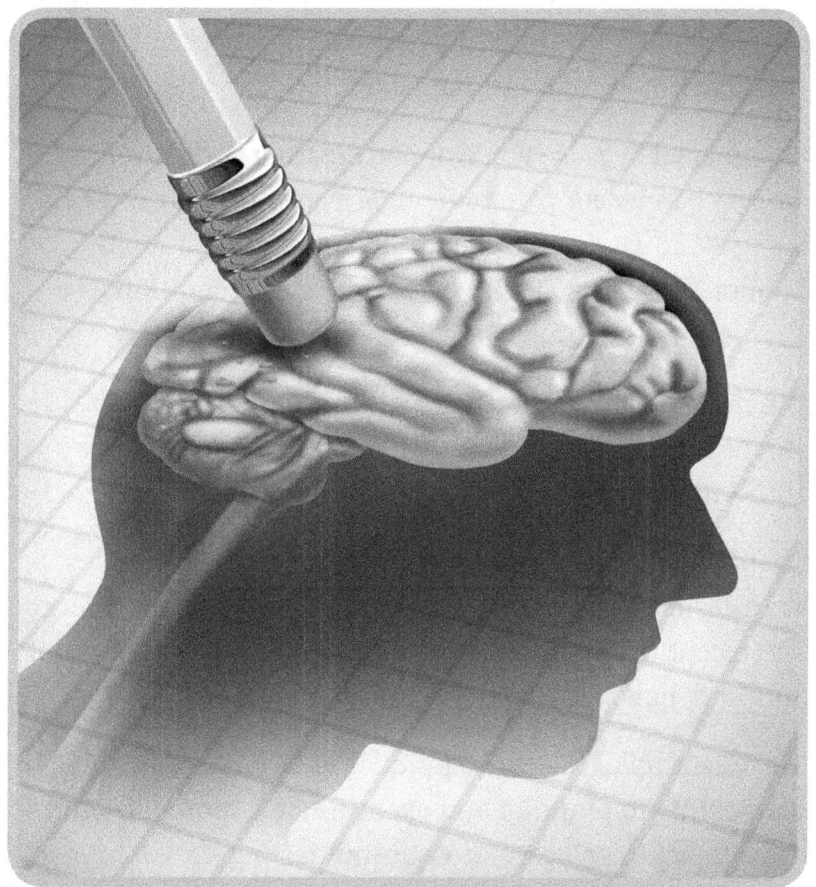

What does Cognitive Optimization look like in practice?

We measure progress in Cognitive Optimization by "Moments of Cognition." When you see clearly that you've been creating a redundant recording of some previous moment or memory, you stop doing it. You cease creating it. And, it vanishes.

When that comes about, there's a moment of "instant emptiness," when the mental recording of that charged moment disappears. It goes "Poof!" Then, heat, warmth, release, laughter, a smile, a pause, and a moment of wonderment at what just happened.

It happened because you stopped creating it. It had already happened. You remember it as much as need be, but you had also been re-creating it as a Sub-Rational Memory, investing it with high amounts of emotional charge because it was "so important."

When you realized it wasn't that important, and stopped compulsively re-creating it, it erased. (And the Sub-Rational Mind becomes just that much smaller.)

That moment of erasure is the defining aspect of the Transformative Dialogue. You release your pent-up energy and recapture an increment of attention back from eternal Sub-Rational captivity.

The intention of the entire practice is to gain confidence in your ability to pinpoint and examine such moments, and erase them, in an ever more substantial degree. Of course, there are significant milestones in case reduction, and in the speed and assurance you gain in moving forward, re-capturing energy, insight, assurance and certainty of your own regained abilities.

Counseling—Holding the Space

"Great Listening is Engaged Receptivity."
—James P. Carse

"Counseling" is a "Suspect Practice" in my mind.

All those people who went to school to "get certified" to tell me how to think. Or to endlessly enquire "How do you feel about that?" Then to (perhaps forcibly) medicate me if I'm not feeling what they intend. Strikes me as about the most useless way to spend an hour.

So this is a tough sell.

But I'm beginning to get the sense that Holosophy Counseling is different, in a good way. You guys seem less interested in telling me what to think or feel, than in helping me...

> figure out how to sort out my own mental real estate. But tell me more.
>
> I'd like a better sense about what makes "this Counseling" different than the people who give "Mental Health" a bad name.

Counseling: It's not just listening, but listening without reacting, judging or evaluating. What we need isn't someone to sympathize, or tell us "There, there, it's not your fault."

What is required is a non-emotional, neutral dialogue with someone who can guide us as we progressively inventory our own case, and systematically expose and resolve all the life incidents that have served to carry accumulated stress and hurl us periodically and unconsciously back in time.

With each incident resolved, cognitive capacity is increased, and calm, insight and perception are enhanced. The work is done inside, focusing on Sub-Rational content, but also outside, in the ongoing, objective dialogue. As the incidents are called up, identified and resolved, the redundant material dissolves, and ordinary memory and cognition re-assert themselves.

You can't "solve this" or "do this" for someone else. But you can act as an ally in the process and remind them not to get "lost in the files" as they work through an incident. You can also encourage them not to quit if it gets unnerving. The best analogy for a Counselor is an attentive, stable, objective anchor — who's not going away until a (your) satisfactory conclusion is reached.

The Counselor stays fully present in the moment, centered and constant, holding the space while the client goes in, digs around, comes back, talks about their discoveries, cognites, then pauses to breathe and consider.

Providing this service requires a "constancy and stability" of viewpoint that is very special and rare. So while Counselor Duties might seem basic: explaining the task at hand, indicating the beginning and end of an exercise, assessing results, the greatest service is creating the safe place for the client to take on the endeavor, and holding the space while they work.

Counselor: One who listens, holds the space, and provides a neutral backstop against which the client can evaluate their own cognitive achievements.

Opening Questions

A Holosophy Counselor helps you objectively take stock of your life, your values, your stories and your ways of interacting with the world. Together, in the context of the dialogue, you can hold up one aspect of life at a time to sober evaluation.

1. What worries you most about the future?

2. Are you holding onto something that you need to let go of?

3. What's the difference between living and existing?

4. If we learn from our mistakes, why are we always so afraid to make a mistake?

5. What impact do you want to leave on the world?

6. Is it out of reach, or have you just not stretched yourself far enough?

7. In the haste of our daily lives, what are we not seeing?

8. If life is so short, why do we do so many things we don't like and like so many things we don't do?

9. If you looked into the heart of your enemy, what do you think you would find that is different from what is in your own heart?

10. If you haven't achieved it yet, what do you have to lose?

11. Why do you matter?

12. How many of your friends would you trust with your life?

13. Are you happy with yourself?

14. What do you do with the majority of your money?

15. Based on your current daily actions and routines, where do you see yourself in five years?

16. What have you done that you are not proud of?

17. Other than money, what else have you gained from your current job?

18. What is the number one change you need to make in your life in the next 12 months?

19. In what way are you your own worst enemy?

20. What do you wish you didn't know?

21. What have you given up on?

22. What big lesson could people learn from your life?

23. What mistakes do you make over and over again?

24. What has been draining your happiness?

25. What's the #1 thing you intend to accomplish before you die?

26. What has the little voice inside your head been saying lately?

27. What is worse than death?

28. What's one easy way to waste a life?

29. How short would your life have to be before you would start living differently?

Mind as Lens

"You cannot have a positive life and a negative mind."
—Joyce Meyer

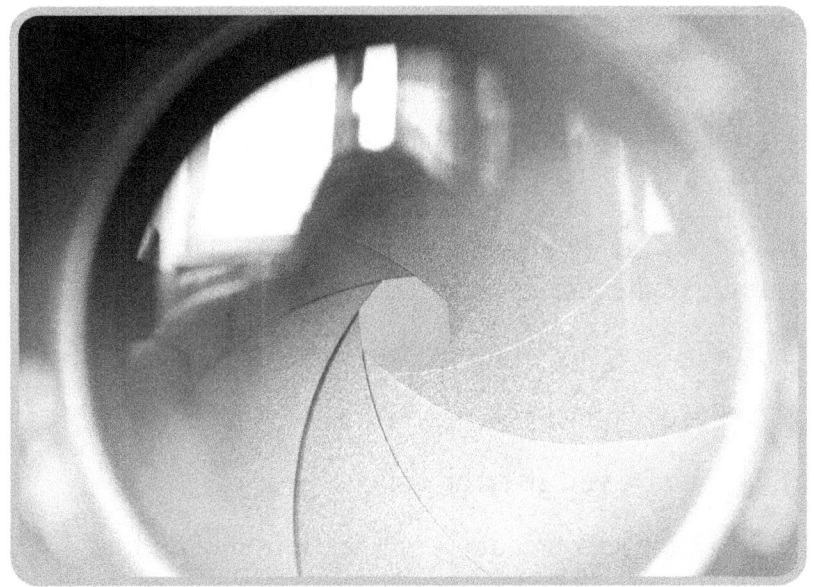

The mind is an "organ of perception" and external events can leave a "reflexive mark" as the organ tends to not only perceive an external event, but also interpret and anticipate based on previous experience.

Just as a Lens can be ground to a certain specific "degree of refraction," a mind can, through experience, be influenced through trauma into a certain persistent band of perception. Things tend to be seen through a dark filter, and deliver a perception which may not be entirely off-key but not entirely accurate, either.

There lies the nature of Sub-Rational influence. It may not be entirely false, but because it is reflexive and habitual, it may not be entirely open to perceiving the full range of what is actually occurring.

So we are left with a person who always anticipates the worst. Someone who is habitually on guard. Someone who simply can't believe that a good thing is about to happen. The range of Sub-Rational indications is large, as demonstrated in Section One. The mechanism of that reluctance is quite simple: the habitual off-key perception of a mind which has given in to the grinding down of ongoing difficult experience.

The process of Cognitive Optimization is designed to greatly reduce false perception, and to rehabilitate the individual's ability to see things as they are, and as they might become.

Solution: Summary
What is Holosophy?

Holosophy is a new branch of philosophy with a practical focus on solving a unique kind of life-problem of the mind called Success Reluctance.

It is a collection of perspectives, practices, understandings, tests, approaches, tools, collected wisdom and advice.

It is not a religion, but a body of wisdom and practice.

It is not based on faith, but on trial and error over a lifetime of practical application.

The tenets of Holosophy, applied correctly and with sustained commitment, can help one gain substantial control over their own mental processes.

The individual is not the Brain, not the Mind, not the Body, but the Being. Becoming aware of that reality is the first of many great steps forward in Holosophy.

A Holosopher hasn't "solved" everything, but is simply

able to see life more clearly, having removed many challenges to accurate perception.

Holosophy isn't a Solution to Life, but a tool for enhanced perception and better living.

Section 4: Praxis

Holosophy in Practice

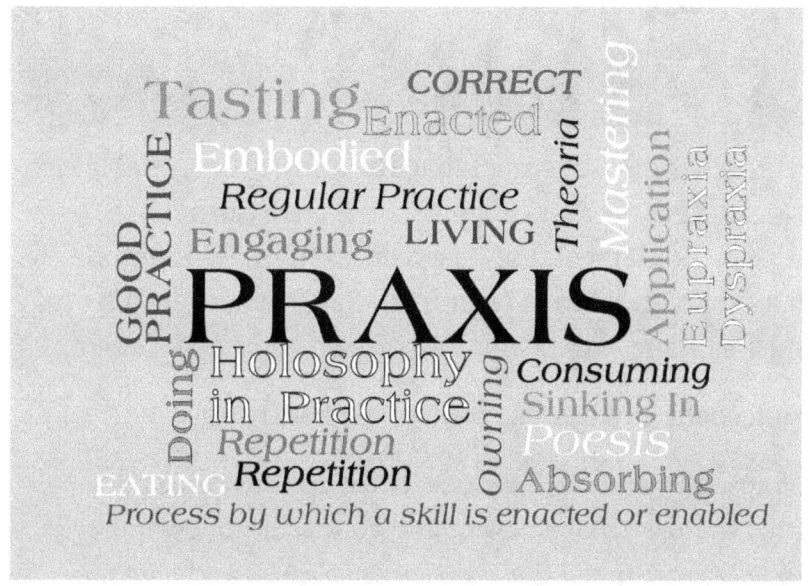

Praxis: Overview

"Praxis: the process by which a theory, lesson or skill is enacted, embodied or realized. 'Praxis' may also refer to the act of engaging, applying, exercising, realizing or practicing ideas... This concept recurs in the philosophical, spiritual and educational realms. Praxis tends to entwine with communication."
—**Wikipedia**

Aristotle suggested that Thinking (Theoria), Making (Poesis) and Doing (Praxis) were the most fundamental of mankind's activities. Eupraxia (Good Practice) and Dyspraxia, (Bad Practice, leading to misfortune) were the final two aspects of the discussion.

Holosophy can be done well, or haphazardly.

Holosophy done as Eupraxia, involves the praxis of interchange between client and counselor: one who seeks improvement; and one who seeks to assist and teach. Good Praxis involves serious initial study, getting a deep sense of what's at issue, establishing a solid understanding of the importance and power of clear, unreserved communication; then a regular and relaxed shifting between Counsel and Tutorial. Then steadily pursuing the next stage of personal growth.

Hannah Arendt discussed Praxis as an exercise of adoption which required "tasting" a skill, an idea, a perspective — a personal, physical demonstration and absorption of learning.

In this sense, we suggest that Holosophy is best undertaken not as something one merely reads about, talks about; or thinks about, but as something that one actively, personally **engages**. Dive in, explore, argue, discover and be touched, influenced and forever changed and enhanced. Taste! And, metabolize.

A lifetime of Holosophy practice (because of its unique "negative gain" aspect) does not **add** to one's burdens, but **reduces the load** as insight is expanded.

Habits of Practice

"Best Practices can be discovered, evolved and formalized.
In every undertaking, there are better ways to operate,
and some that are less, well, 'Professional.'
In any case, 'Do No Harm!' is a great starter.
Then, move on to 'Serve the Client First.'
Finally, 'Remain Quiet and Neutral!'
Your job is not to share an opinion, but to
'Hold the Space' as the client forms their own."
—Holosophy Canon

"You know, I make it a point to share my case, and my case progress with my kids, my spouse, my business partner, my mom, my analyst and my colleagues at work. "The More, the Merrier!", I say.

And of course, everyone has an opinion, a suggestion, and a curious interest in how I'm doing. (But I wonder, "Do they all have the same interest in my individual progress?")

> I want to maximize the return on my Counseling Investment. So I arrive early, to "share the returns" on last week, then get busy with this week's issues, then finish by laying out how I think everyone might react to this week's revelations. That way, my Counselor and I can see how his strategy is working out among all the constituents.
>
> I saw this approach once on Reality TV. It seemed like a great way to get help and good advice for everyone in the cast, and everyone seemed to learn a lot! And hey, it's a great way to spread the good investment around."
>
> [This may be the perfect example of real life Dyspraxia, leading ultimately to misfortune.]

As we embark on the process of Cognitive Optimization through the tool of the Transformative Dialogue, some general advice for students and practitioners presents itself:

This is not a dental appointment. Nor the kind with an Attorney or a Therapist. Nor is it a "Reality Television" show.

This is a free-wheeling discussion of the Perennial Philosophy and the great questions, along with a deep dive into your own views, assumptions and concerns about life and living. Then comes exploring your deep case — the un-inspected collection of related dark incidents which comprise your unique "Sub-Rational mind." You take this on in order to resolve your problems, and expand your view of the universe.

1. Be on Time. This is about respecting yourself, and not letting the case interfere in the process of growth. ("Electing to Be Late" is a standard, but not very lofty barrier to a successful process.)

2. Keep in mind that Counsel should be undertaken by someone who is well fed, rested and clean of artificial forms of interference.

3. Don't "share" your session information. It invites your case (then everyone else's case) to form an opinion and place a vote — on your private endeavor. It's hard enough to put your feelings and concerns out there to be examined and considered. When there are "others" also involved in the process by remote control, it only makes the entire exercise more difficult, less free and not at all spontaneous. After all, just who is being counseled here?

4. Be Forthcoming! Don't hold back your questions, comments, doubts, criticisms, concerns, fears or hidden intentions. Sometimes, people elect to keep their thoughts about the process or the counselor, to themselves. This has the unfortunate effect of keeping the real issues away from the Dialogue where they can be addressed and handled. The more you hold back, the more Case is unavailable for handling. Get it out in the open where you and your Counselor can "See Whatever It Is, As It Truly Is." When you withhold yourself from the process, it really can't benefit you.

5. "Let the Cognition Breathe." As you have a new awareness, you might "Clamp it down and file it away for later analysis. On the other hand, you might allow the moment of new awareness to "air itself out across the domains." This approach might expand both the depth and breadth of the cognition, at no extra charge. Never hesitate to share that moment and laugh at the nature of self-delusion. It inoculates you against the next mistake.

6. **"Keep a Journal.*"** This is a lifetime undertaking. Give it thought. Become aware of your thinking, your patterns and your chosen limitations. As your insights grow, so will the span of your case. It's just as smart as you are. So your notes are a powerful way of documenting your own progress, and helping you set a course for further discovery and discussion. Looking back on your cognitive improvement can also give you a sense of reality to share when you one day become a counselor.

*See *The Red Book* by **Carl Jung.**

Catching Your "Self"

Stephen Falken: "General, what you see on these screens up here is a fantasy, a computer-enhanced hallucination. Those blips are not real missiles. They're phantoms."

McKittrick: "Jack, there's nothing to indicate a simulation at all. *Everything is working perfectly!*"

Stephen Falken: "*But does it make any sense?*"
- *War Games*

How do you know you've descended into the Sub-Rational realm?

There are a variety of behavioral/intellectual indicators, which recur in the presence of Sub-Rational thinking:

- Anger
- Guilt
- Misery
- Habitual or addictive behavior

- Hyper-Criticality (Hidden standards of expectation)
- Outrage
- Martyrdom
- Individuation, separation from one's support group
- Blaming

The list is too numerous to include.*

In the years to come, you'll encounter moments like this fictional portrayal, where a young man's insight into what he considers "obvious" encounters fierce resistance from everyone else — all of whom are **committed to a shared illusion**.

If this were easy, you'd simply read the book and go about your business, pop into a new loftier level of consciousness, and never have another dip into the Sub-Rational.

But then, our real lives are fraught with challenge, upset, confusion — the things that make us unsteady, force us to miss appointments, to mis-estimate our strength (or someone else's). We make mistakes, bump into things and start "following our instincts," re-acting, jumping to conclusions, and all of a sudden, we're back where we started. At the bottom of a deep hole, with our friends, lovers and family peering over the edge, wondering where and how we disappeared.

Because our cases **make so much sense**, to us!

Sometime soon, you'll find yourself arguing *for* your mental case:

"Look, I have to do this. I know you guys are worried

about me. I know I'm cutting ties with everyone I've ever loved or trusted. I know you all think I'm crazy, but this is what I have to do!"

You could be right. It's the chance of a lifetime! Or, it could be crazy. (It could be your case talking to you…)

Fortunately, there are objective tools available, which help us identify and evaluate the truth of many viewpoints: our own, and others. Being able to critique any position objectively gives us a distinct advantage over mere habit or opinion. In the end, *we have to catch ourselves*.

The ultimate question: **"But does it make any sense?"**

* The entire reference catalog of Sub-Rational Indicators is available
from the
Holosophy Foundation.

Shelf Space

"In the supermarket, there's a noisy and expensive war going on between Brand A and Brand X. Brand A is the favorite, and they have the money to protect their position, so they spend a lot of it renting the most valuable shelf space: precisely at eye level! And the truth holds: Whatever is seen repeatedly at center stage, SELLS!

"Whether in the supermarket or the marketplace of ideas; Whether it's a soft drink, a mutual fund or any idea; it won't get anywhere without exposure to your attention — shelf space! The supermarket is an easy and obvious metaphor. The media marketplace is a cultural infestation of noise, propaganda and promotion — all contending for a particle of your attention. But 'Shelf-Space in the Mind' is a 'market' of much greater importance and wholly subject to your personal interests and desires."

— Jennifer StJohn

Look at me. I'm a mess! I can't pay my bills. I'm fighting with my boyfriend. I'm not talking with my mother. My husband left me. My place is a mess. The city wants to turn off my water. My car is barely running. The world has it in for me! See!

Holosophy - Conquering Your Fear of Success

> My dog hates me! The kids are in revolt. Work is in a state of collapse.
>
> I'm not at fault! Things are just totally messed up! How am I supposed to improve or change my life with all this chaos?
>
> I think God has it in for me. My life is over.

Here's a concept: your thoughts and interests are yours to create, manage and promote.

Ever had a day when the synapses just don't fire, the neurons seem clogged and constricted, the eyes can't quite focus and the mind is foggy? The internal landscape seems curiously unreal and the external landscape, well... Outsiders seem like enemies, and insiders seem like interruptions just waiting to occur!!

That's the Sub-Rational mind — infringing on the available mental shelf space. A problem demanding your attention. A lens that requires cleaning. A viewpoint that has become occluded. An old upset that, over time, becomes a trusted friend.

It remains, and grows, but only if it's given space.

Cognitive Optimization is "Thinking Better." More clearly, more cleanly, with no inappropriate overtones. Emotion is reasonable, of course, except when it moves in, hangs around and demands accommodation. It's an act of will, but your life depends entirely on you, and the space you choose to make available out of your limited supply to whatever idea or perspective you deem valuable.

There are big ideas, there are small ones, destructive ones, critical ones, a sense of victimhood or a sense of adventure. Whatever you choose to put "right there at eye level" will claim your attention, and your life.

Choose carefully, and Decide which idea and which viewpoint will get shelf space in your mind.

One Stanza

"Do not confuse understanding with a larger vocabulary. Sacred writings are beneficial in stimulating desire for inward realization, but only if one stanza at a time is slowly assimilated. Continual intellectual study results in vanity and the false satisfaction of undigested knowledge."
—**Sri Yukteswar Giri**

So how does one study Holosophy? How shall I go about acquiring more information, wisdom, practical application? Which books shall I buy? Which shall I read first? How soon can I begin to levitate? When will I be promoted to leadership?

Slow down there; it's a big undertaking! Especially if you propose to do it all at once, and all in one shot.

One stanza. One sentence. The steady, rhythmic "puh-ping" of the chisel against the granite of our misunderstanding…

Spiritual wisdom, penetration, discernment, perception, intelligence does not come all at once, but instead is acquired in bits, in small flashes of insight.

As you read, you will acquire new words, new contexts, new perspectives and new understandings. As you take a bite of the new information, you'll get an initial insight, but then you'll return to your daily program... But as you review your session, you may realize an aspect of the teaching that was not immediately apparent, and the cognition will expand.

The next session, you'll propose questions based on what you've already studied. And the new perspective, enjoyed as a result of a further discussion, will begin to settle in and establish a new boundary of understanding. The following week, you'll read another passage, and consider how it relates to what you now know. A discussion with another student will change your focus and perspective and leave you with more questions for the Counselor. As you pursue these areas in your session, more insight will become available.

One day, sitting at a cafe table on the street, you'll be thinking about your studies and the entire city will become brighter somehow, and your breath will stop as a particular insight reveals itself. In that moment, the world may stop turning for you, as an aspect of your life, the universe, Holosophy and existence becomes clear in a new way. And it will all happen exactly on schedule.

Then, as things return to their daily rhythms, you'll return to your studies, changed and the same. You'll see more deeply, be more compassionate, and yet more yourself.

And the cycle repeats...

"Puh-Ping! Puh-Ping! Puh-Ping!"

I Won't Trance!

"I won't trance
You can't make me
I won't sleep
You won't wake me!"
(with apologies to **Frank Sinatra.**)

I'm not so wild about the idea of sitting in a chair, laying on a couch, sitting on the floor; and staring into space.

And I'm not a "good" subject.

I don't like the whole idea of giving up control.

You get this? This is my life here; and I'm the Boss!

So just what is it that you propose to do, and

> how is it accomplished?
>
> And be careful! No sudden moves!
> I'm watching!

Contemporary culture seems to call out for drugs. Alcohol dulls the senses and distances one from the unremitting daily confront. Marijuana softens the edges, and brings a smile. And of course, there are sixty-six daily commercials touting medications for maladies like depression, weight gain, asthma, allergies — each with a softly, swiftly-spoken, legal brief, outlining the potential hazards.

Oh, and don't operate heavy machinery.

A common aspect of the many New Age Help Modalities is their reliance on some form of "Trance." As a precondition for being helped, you must first reduce your consciousness to a less acute level. Submit to Hypnosis. Dial back. Go to Sleep. Check out.

Or, take the Express and Go "Full Medical!" Have a technician insert the needle and pump you full of sedatives. To be followed afterwards with regular, timed doses of narcotics. Relax, it's all covered.

We differ…

To Holosophy, the idea that progress might be defined by reducing consciousness, or adding a drug or a post-hypnotic suggestion, is — quite simply — backward. We suggest that anything that genuinely helps can be undertaken while fully aware and awake, on one's own determinism.

As we see it, the problem isn't that you don't have enough drugs, treatment, programming, or trance. It's that you have too much. You're already overwhelmed.

The solution *isn't* going into a deeper trance. **It's gradually, but steadily, waking up!**

Holosophy Counseling is about becoming really conscious of what you've been doing, what you are doing unconsciously; then ceasing to do it.

We think it's a benefit to have a Counselor to assist with staying on track, focusing the discussion and being an objective witness. Our commitments to our own crazy perceptions are harder to maintain when we try to explain them to an objective listener. If it looks or sounds crazy, you know; it probably is.

That and an understanding of the ways in which we camouflage our commitments to our own limitations is all that's required.

No drugs. No sleep. No trance. No added suggestions on top of those from last week, last upset, last trauma. Let's make the pile smaller, shall we?

So, as attractive as more drugs, hypnosis, treatment referrals are, I won't take the chance.

Doggone it, I just won't, trance!

The State of Things

"Few people seem so safe as someone
with whom we've shared a confidence."
—Jennifer StJohn

Most people have experienced nothing quite like the Transformative Dialogue, nor do they understand its Protocols or Standards of Practice.

Suffice to say that one does not begin by simply demanding that the client offer up the worst moment of their life for examination.

Instead, there is a gentle process of establishing a connection, outlining the Cognitive Optimization process, its objectives and practices and answering preliminary questions.

Then, we begin by taking stock and "Establishing the

State of Things." This involves getting a survey of what's in question, where it hurts, what's in a state of immediate need, and through this early discussion, building the trust, confidence and ease with the personal interplay that makes the client confident that they can "tell the counselor anything."

This also allows the counselor a sense of what's at issue and a brief time to foresee the needs, and plan pathways for exploration.

There's no rule for how we do this; but in general, we start by getting familiar with the other person, then with the issues they bring to the meeting and finally with Holosophy Practices. As the dialogue progresses, we are faced with a series of choices: A or B? B or C? Break until next session. Each meeting, the process remains very similar, but the issues change with the circumstances.

(See also: Counsel/Tutorial page 159)

Talk, Learn, Laugh!
(Repeat!)

"Talking helps by taking something that's really difficult in here,
and moving it out there where I can look at it
without having to wear it!"
—Robert Benjamin

How is Holosophy Done? It's a lot of things. But the practice of it, in session, well, that's a dialogue. Not a free association. Not an un-directed wandering.

In fact, it's very specific.

After all, much — if not most — of your life is working just fine! It's the parts that aren't working quite so well that are of interest.

So that's where we begin. The client and a counselor "Survey the Case" together, and make a list: "Areas of Interest. Areas of Concern."

Then we prioritize; and begin the dialogue.

What about this area seems at issue? Where does it hurt? What about it seems to be important? When does this come up? Do you remember a time when it first came up?

Holosophy is a series of directed discussions about life, with special focus on where things aren't working, and then following those areas down to their origins in the collection of ancient hurt that we call the Sub-Rational realm. Each of us has a store of conclusions, considerations, character traits and concerns that define us. Some of them are so highly charged that they tend to overpower our own reason in difficult situations. Those powerful historical concerns are what we look for in a session.

Once exposed, we are able to look closely at an area and allow the client to see it in a new moment. To decide how important this area seems now. Maybe it was pretty important back then, but things have changed. They have changed, haven't they? And that's the nature of a new awareness, and the release of the underlying concern about something that allows the client to move on.

It's that simple. We talk.

We discover that what was a big deal then, may not be such a big deal now.

The Whole of It!

"So when you're listening to somebody, completely, attentively, then you are listening not only to the words, but also to the feeling of what is being conveyed, to the whole of it, not part of it."

—Jiddu Krishnamurti

As a Counselor, there's a pressure at the beginning, to show your stuff, to solve the problem, to demonstrate your insight... There's a huge urge to talk... which we must resist. We often don't realize that this thing we do — the dialogue — is much more subtle than simply being silent — although that's a terrific start...

The real thing we're doing, is watching (and positively intending) as the individual surveys the situation from the other side of the fortress she's erected around her feelings. At some point, she makes a decision: "OK, I'll risk it!" Moments (or minutes) later, she shifts in her chair a little and starts to think about the words to express her feelings. She will make a small attempt — then see if you react — then play to the reaction — at which point the thing is off track. Don't rise to the bait. Listen — don't react. When you don't react, she decides it's safe. She says a few more things, with greater confidence. And then, the dialogue begins to "bite!"

Nobody puts everything on the table at once. Nobody puts it out there at first. We're all too smart for that.

You have to wait for it. You have to let them do it. You're listening for the "Whole of It!"

So there's a lot there, under the surface. There's *what* happened. There's *what they think* happened. There's *what they hope* happened. There's the *feelings they had* running up to what happened, The feelings they had afterward. The *feelings they had about the feelings*. The outcome(s). Other people's perspective about all of the above.

A case is like a little fish, inside a bigger fish, inside a yet bigger fish, inside a shark, wrapped in a fishing net, inside a whale, dragging a harpoon float. With a whaling ship — all sails aloft — in close pursuit.

That's the "Whole of it." So when you're listening, wait for it — there's more. Count on it!

Your job is not to leap to any obvious conclusions about any of it, not to judge, not to react but to provide an objective, safe place for the client to bring all of that to the surface and deal with it — in their own time.

Great Counselors seem almost inert — they are present — but not acting or re-acting. Engaged receptivity.

"Listening for the Whole of It."

New Awareness

"The most difficult part of our practice is dealing with our habit-ridden consciousness."
—Hakuin

That moment when you become aware that you've been carrying around duplicates of every harsh experience. Just to be sure you remember. Wouldn't want to venture out unprepared for whatever happens. But as you begin the journey of Cognitive Optimization, in the dialogue, something will "pop." A new awareness! "Hey, That's an unnecessary (even redundant) memory. I can let it go…" And there we have it: Cognition!

You look again, and, it's gone! You still know it happened, there's still an awareness. But that heavy file of pain, fear, upset, agony, sadness and heavy pictures; you know, the baggage. Gone! Erased!

That's what we seek to create: Moments of Cognition, in an endless series.

New awarenesses — moments in which old, redundant thoughts are revealed as nothing more than freighted, emotional overlays, and, as a result — vanish.

Habits of Clarity

"To read without reflecting is like eating without digesting."
—Edmund Burke

A "cognition" is a moment of enhanced awareness, when intense focus on an issue succeeds in erasing one or more false constructs — and you perceive more clearly. Due to the inter-related quality of the Sub-Rational mind, it is only natural that you might say to yourself, "Wait a second, if that's true, (and that is not) then, what about that?" If you sustain your focus on the area, the false inter-related structures begin to wobble a bit under your gaze. "And the walls come tumbling down."

That's the way it should happen. And it often does.

Then, sometimes, it doesn't. Why?

We're pretty serious about our case. Remember, it's a cross-referenced web of feelings, emotions, sensations, thoughts, experiences and conclusions. And it's more than that, because it has been gathered together during moments of stress — so this stuff is important. Really!

So we might be forgiven for holding onto it all with an unusual fervency. "It's kept us alive all this time!" Right?

But from time to time we hit the trifecta: getting a good moment of recognition, then a few moments later, the second domino falls and finally the uncontrolled laughter, signaling an entire region, a "Web" of Sub-Rational connections, caving in. The rest of the day is often punctuated by a series of related giggles, smiles, snorts and sighs as we slowly dismantle an entire neighborhood of Sub-Rational constructs. With each cognition, we take back more cognitive capacity — and our certainty grows.

So make it a point to cultivate a few Habits of Clarity.

1. Take time to let a cognition sink in and spread. Don't be in a hurry for the next big breakthrough. Savor the newly won territory!

2. Pause afterward and ask yourself, "Is this part of a larger construct? Have I been relying on this line of thinking to defend, preserve, obscure something I deem important? Is it really what I want? Is it really me?"

3. Notice that there is often a "Rear Guard" that sets in immediately after a cognition: a self-limiting intention to minimize the reach and extent of the new awareness. Catch that in action and you're on the way to another big gain.

Ok, Do Me!

"American materialism has affected the spiritual path deeply—manifesting in seeking magical states, instant gratification, and a shallow, results-driven spirituality. Genuine search places us in the eye of the tiger. It is raw and an anathema to our ego. It demands rigor and discipline, and the striving towards impartial self-observation which brings in its train a certain kind of suffering and discomfort. Genuine spiritual growth is fundamentally transformative, not merely a rearrangement of our personalities or an increased ability to meet the demands of life. It is learning to serve a different master, our search for higher consciousness and for the awakening of conscience, and placing our ego or our conditioned personality in a secondary, not primary, role."
—**David Ulrich**

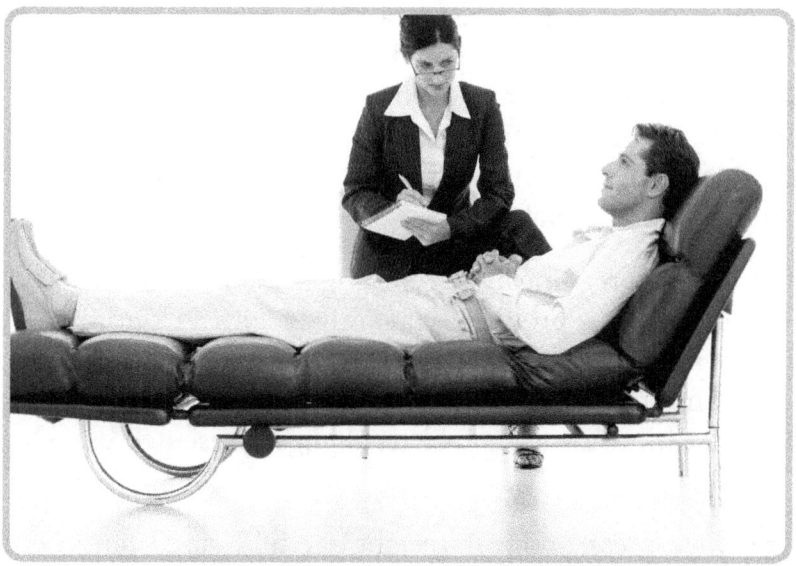

Ok, I'm ready! I've been looking for the answer, and I'm just sure that This is It!

I know how this works! So I'm heading for the couch, laying down and getting ready for you to count down, get me out and get me clear of all my neuroses!
Hit me!

Holosophy - Conquering Your Fear of Success

> Trance me! Drug me! Hypnotize me! I'm ready! I'm set. I know all about this stuff, and I'm totally with it! I've got a set of Arcosanti bells on my porch, a personal Mantra, an Exercise Coach and a Diet Guru. I've got a wardrobe of yoga pants with matching mats, and a complete library of Baba Ram Dass!
>
> So what are we waiting for? Let's Go!

Perhaps you misunderstand. Holosophy is not something done to you. Instead it is a study which you undertake, at your own pace and discretion. The process of Cognitive Optimization begins with the consideration that things CAN get better, but only if you choose to make it so!

You begin by reading and absorbing the concepts and practices. As you progress, you affiliate with a Counselor and engage the Transformational Dialogue. There are steps, and stops along the way while you identify and wrestle with the innumerable challenges presented by the case.

As you progress, and gain insight into how cases, (and your unique case) are constructed; you begin to gain familiarity and sophistication in identifying and erasing "things" which had earlier appeared insoluble.

But to be clear, Holosophy can't be "done to you" or "for you." Instead, it is a program of self-study and cultivation which makes use of a Counselor Coach to provide objective signposts to direct and measure progress.

It's yours. But we can help you handle it!

Assume You're Wrong

"The most erroneous stories are those we think we know best, and therefore never scrutinize or question."
—Stephen Jay Gould

So, I'm pretty capable! Darned articulate, good looking, kind, loving and a really excellent golfer.

I'm excelling in my career and I have an insight into life that my friends find very helpful.

My taste is beyond reproach.

Now that you mention it, I'm quite a scholar and can find the hole in any argument!

What makes you think you have anything to teach me?

Of all the things we know for sure, our own feelings, attitudes, and perspectives are our most cherished and unquestioned possessions. And for that reason, they are suspect.

A lot of mistakes go by unnoticed because they are hiding inside our collection of unquestioned truths.

Holosophy suggests that it's a good thing to rely on more than "feel" or "familiarity" to assess the truth or utility of an idea, a perspective, a practice or an understanding.

What about submitting such things to an objective test?

How many times have we been with an able partner or friend who tells us, "Hey, you're behaving a little outside the realm of polite conversation here. Are you perhaps losing your mind? Having a little sub-rational moment?"

And we of course, say, "Why No! I'm as sober as a judge and rational as a logician in a watch factory! Leave me alone!" And we continue on our merry way — alienating friends, family members and co-workers along the way.

Is it so difficult to hear and act responsibly when people advise us that we might be wrong? Is there something about being mistaken occasionally that we just can't face? Is our pride so important? Must we always endure the bloody collision of our self-confidence with reality? (And the destruction of friendships, working relationships and even our marriages in order to wake up to our predilection for rightness at all costs?)

Why can't we just assume we're wrong from time to time and check our "Assumption File" for that one unquestionable premise? What does it cost us to stop and check to see if we were a little (or a lot) off base?

Holosophy's best advice as you start the path of Cognitive Optimization: Be willing to check your assumptions, question your judgment and ask yourself just one more time; "Am I on point here? Have I got everything right? Or should I step back and get a second opinion?" Add a side order of humility as you walk the path of enlightenment.

It costs but a few moments, and it might save your job, your marriage or your best friend. The reason we rely on the Holosophy Dialogue, is that it provides us the one thing we can't get for ourselves: Objectivity!

The Transformative Dialogue provides space, time and a coach: allowing you to check your pride at the door and look carefully at what you're thinking, saying or "selling."

Indicators
(How do we recognize Sub-Rationality?)

There are "Hints" in the moods.
"Indications" in the language.
"Tells" in the behavior.
We are, all of us, transparent.

So I'm going along just fine here. Nothing wrong. Just "pensive." I keep my thoughts and feelings to myself, take a little longer getting home from work to allow for stopping off at a bar, a club, a friend's house...

Just to allow me a little break from being "perfect" all the time...

What do you mean, "I seem upset?"

We are transparent. Our moods and behavior give away our thoughts and our modes of perception. There's a "tone, or a frequency" attached to every thought and feeling. "Anger" is Darker,

"Love" is Lighter, but substantial. "Affection" is light yet not passionate. "Despair" is a long way down there, and very dim…

Having encountered the broad Ranges and differing Frequencies available in human interaction, we have begun to accumulate a list of Indicators, which can serve to guide our attention to debilitating aspects of our own behavior, and that of others, in the attempt to notice when we have fallen into the trap of seeing "through a glass and darkly."

These "Sub-Rational Indicators" are both numerous and subtle, posing as genuine emotional states, but carrying with them a trace of unchanging, dark blame and false attribution for one's unhappy circumstances to life, family, others, the environment, or God. "I'm not doing well, and it's probably someone else's fault!"

Catching one's self in a puddle of Sub-Rational Self-Pity is an initial step in rising from the emotional sub-basement to a norm of rational day-to-day life. Then, rising to the summit of an optimized life are the fundamental goals of Holosophy study and practice.

Cognitive Optimization is the process of becoming self-aware of one's own indicators, with the ultimate goal of resolving them in the moment as they appear. That state of "instant self-actualization" may be a way off for most of us, but "noticing the indicator when it appears," is the first step in Cognitive Optimization.

Sub-Rational Indicators
(available as a complete booklet from the Holosophy Foundation)

The indicators list is comprised of eight subcategories: Criticalness, Continuity, Confusion, Dis-Interest, Dis-Ability, Generality, Mis-Emotion and Mis-Perception. The following list defines just a few of the indicators, (from the Mis-Emotion Category) for illustrative purposes.

"**Alienation**" a withdrawing or distancing oneself from things or persons of former attachment; self-exile or "loner-ism" often tinged with self-pity, wounded-ness, numbness or the steely resolve to be invulnerable to the "pain" of disappointment or betrayal.

"**Boredom**" an unpleasant state of being irresponsibly devoid of interest.

"**Covert Hostility**" a secret or hidden unfriendliness, injurious-ness or ill will; antagonism, opposition or resistance in thought or action.

"**Degradation**" a shameful or humiliating sense of diminished or lost status, rank, or worth.

"**Hopelessness**" a state of having no expectation of ultimate good or success, of not being susceptible to remedy or cure, of being incapable of solution, management or accomplishment.

Who has not felt, at times, distanced from family or peers? Who has not felt boredom or a moment of hopelessness? True. But the distinction with Sub-Rational indicators is that they persist — taking up more and more mental real-estate, and interfering with life to a degree far beyond their momentary importance. For most of us, a bad feeling is a normal part of life, but "normal" means that bad feelings don't persist, not for hours, certainly not for days, and absolutely not for weeks!

Sub-Rational Indicators are "symptoms," showing us where an individual requires attention to resolve underlying case issues.

The subsequent chapters in this section provide a variety of detailed examples of the kinds of real-life situations where Success Reluctance manifests, though it may remain unnoticed, for a moment, or a lifetime…

The Indicators are an ever-present clue, and an implicit suggestion for focused cognitive optimization.

Constructing Victimhood

"What does a god experience least?
Being a Victim..."

"If scarcity increases the value of a thing;
Victimhood might seem remarkably important!"
—Joshua Wellerby

Being a "Victim" requires a "Villain." Somebody to blame for this wholly untenable situation! And all of that means you must pretend that you *can* be a victim, and that it could ever be someone else's fault.

It's like a Template for a Personal Morality Play...

Good Guy, Bad Guy, Extenuating Circumstances.

Crushing, Un-confrontable Evil.

And, a long suffering victim...

But in order for it to be convincing, you have to pretend really hard that you aren't in charge, didn't know, couldn't see, can't be stage-managing the whole thing in order to avoid responsibility.

And that much pretense requires that someone must be "preternaturally stupid!" Are you that stupid? Really? Are you sure you're not just really smart, able and just a little deluded about having been completely, stone solid taken for a ride? Are you getting a little too much pleasure out of all this suffering?

What would happen if you paused, and decided to — just for a moment — consider that this — this whole ugly situation — is **your** handiwork?

Are you sure you're not complicit here? Really? Try it.

See if things improve. And don't suppress the giggle when you figure it out.

Revealed Pretense

"Are we really happy here, with this lonely game we play,
looking for words to say.
Searching but not finding understanding anywhere,
we're lost in a masquerade."
—**Leon Russell** & **Onika Tanya Maraj**
Copyright: Money Mack Music

Premise: We are all-knowing beings, pretending not to know, in order to enjoy the game.

When the pretense is playfully, benevolently, artfully revealed, the players appear momentarily absurd... and the laughter begins.

Children in Adult's clothing? or Adults in Children's clothing?

There is a moment of explosive awareness as the two universes collide and the duplicate collapses. Cue laughter and rueful smiles.

And the game continues.

When we engage the Holosophy dialogue, we tiptoe around the edges of our assumptions and considerations — things we believe to be true. The closer we get to the center, the more tenuous our constructs become. And... at some point, the pretense is revealed. It's all a Game! Our trumped-up self images and all our universes constructed of gossamer dust slowly collapse.

What is there to do but laugh and enjoy this cosmic joke?

"If not for laughter."

Can this find application?

1. For You

Have you ever tried to convince someone that you're a victim? That you're hurt by their spiteful bad temper? (While actually knowing that this entire scene is just a feint to gain advantage?) Shame on you! Laugh and move on.

2. Family

Ever catch your partner thinking she's seventeen? Fantasizing about that summer afternoon? Missing the smoothness of her skin and the pleasure of that sunset? Don't crush the moment! Honor it with a long caress and a shared smile as the pretense fades to reality. You're both here, on the other end of a life together. Perhaps it's not as smooth now, but you built every particle of this together.

Honor each other's pretenses, and grant each other space to be the people you've become. And a giggle at that youthful exuberance is OK too.

3. Work/Community

Your Boss wants to Rule the World! In his dreams! Let him! Get in the sand box for a second with feeling! Then smile and comment about that lack of front line soldiers to enact his vision. Let him laugh and get back to getting this shipment out the door.

Adults? Children? Perhaps they're the same. Lost in the Masquerade.

(But if we're aware of it, we can enjoy it and laugh at it at the same time.)

Looking Out

"The Native State of a Rational Mind
is Silence: Looking Out…"
—Jennifer StJohn

**Is the self "That which watches" or
"That which is being watched?"
It's one of the Great Questions.**

Most of us spend our lifetime living "trapped in the box of our awareness" with the Monkeys, the Elephant, the Mirror, the Voices, the High School Friends, our Parent's Judgements, our Sibling's Criticisms and our Mate's Evaluations. It's a prison of endless, unimaginable abrasion. Being reduced to mere elements.

But all of that is not what or who we are. That's just the noise on the screen. That's just what is being watched. In earlier times, it was called, "The Monkey Mind." But that's not you.

We are (You are) The Watcher. We can (and You can) (eventually) control what we invite into the box, onto the screen, into our consciousness. (And, what we do not.)

A fundamental freedom: To Choose the Focus of Our Attention. But, like any freedom, it's an ability in disguise.

And any ability is nothing without practice.

It's Hard!

"All wish to possess knowledge, but few, comparatively speaking, are willing to pay the price."
—Juvenal

Why is this so hard?

I mean, it's not like an afternoon at the dentist, but I find myself resisting in large and small ways.

I find myself arriving late... all the time. And that's not like me.

I talk all around the issue before zeroing in on an area of concern.

> I get critical of my Counselor... his clothes, his hands, his way of enunciating.
>
> If I'm honest about this, it's as if my mind knows that Holosophy is a good thing, but there's this "mental dragging of feet."

If someone said, "Hey! Let's take the afternoon off and go to the beach. We can hang out, enjoy the sun, and talk about some of the most difficult moments of our lives, over and over, until they vanish! You in?"

Well, that is essentially, the challenge. Sessions are hard, "down to the painful details" projects. They begin with an overview of process, then move into specific case moments and details — viewed repeatedly until a cognition presents itself — then erasure! So it ends in laughter and relief!

But victories only come after some serious sustained looking.

So, unsurprisingly, sensing its end is near, the Sub-Rational mind puts up a fight! It has all your intellect, all your character, strength, and all your creativity and explanatory wit at its disposal.

The million reasons to "do something else today" will present themselves.

The Counselor's worn shoe will begin to grate on your sensibilities.

The room temperature will seem oppressive.

And the process of case review will stretch out to infinity in front of you.

But then, you'll overcome the resistance and begin…

Then, you see through something, and the session ends in a burst of laughter and a silly awareness that this was all of your own creation.

You gain insight and lose an illusion. And the cycle repeats.

Blame & Resistance

Blame (Definition): An act of irrational creation or destruction.
"You shouldn't have done that! You and it should not BE!"

"A person who blames others has not learned their lesson.
A person who blames themselves has begun their lesson.
A person who blames no one, has learned their lesson."
—**Asian Parable**

Blame is resisting what happened and what is, and trying to wish it out of existence — out of your mind — and all memory. Which — is not going to happen.

Why it's dangerous:

In order to blame, you have to give credence to what was before, rather than what is right now. So you're back there. Rather than right here. I don't know anyone who can do that very well, walking around here, with their head in yesterday. In a funny way; "That which you resist; persists."

Because you're keeping it alive in your mind in order to

make sure it never happens again. But it is happening again - because you have it with you right *here.*

How we use it against others:

Maybe it was a family disagreement — a long time ago. But you've not spoken with that individual since. A brother? A sister? Parent? Child? You can go through the entire range of emotions: anger, sadness, guilt, bluster, rightness. But as long as you have that much invested in resisting what was — you can't be fully present for what is. And that is penalizing now in favor of being outraged about then. And this is just a single instance. How many of these are you carrying? And how hard are you unconsciously working at keeping all of them far away — but at the same time — way too close?

All that's about what it does to **you.**

Imagine for a moment how this affects the people in your circle. Those who love you, notice the "fence"— keeping them away from the warm center — so they cannot repeat that terrible long ago event. Those who respect you would like to get closer — but they notice a strange reserve when talking about serious things. So they decide to keep their distance.

You're defending "yourself," and keeping others at a distance. But that "self" died a long time ago, and those you distance today are never going to have a chance.

A Connection

"Oh, the comfort - the inexpressible comfort of feeling safe with a person - having neither to weigh thoughts nor measure words, but pouring them all right out, just as they are, chaff and grain together, certain that a faithful hand will take and sift them, keep what is worth keeping, and with the breath of kindness blow the rest away."
—Dinah Maria Mulock Craik

Connection (Definition):

An **End Point**. A **Base**. A **Linkage** between one point or person and another. "A **Point of Connection**."

Sometimes, a simple connection is all that's required...

The literature is filled with techniques, studies, prescriptions, suggestions, best practice reviews.

Yeah.

And in many cases, the individual is simply crying out for a connection.

Someone, anyone who will simply listen.

So as a Counselor, start there. Cultivate the skill of engaged receptivity.

Be an empty vessel. Allow this person to know that you're not going anywhere.

No judgement. No comment. No opinion. Just interest.

You're on the side of What's Best for All Concerned. which covers a lot of ground.

You're also on the side of getting it all out, and in the center where the Client can see it objectively.

So study, practice, Counsel, but remember; before everything else, what that person needs is a genuine connection.

Presence, Choice, Responsibility

"Man is condemned to be free; because once thrown into the world, he is responsible for everything he does. It is up to you to give [life] meaning."
—Jean-Paul Sartre

"There is an expiry date on blaming your parents for steering you in the wrong direction; the moment you are old enough to take the wheel, responsibility lies with you."
—J.K. Rowling

Well, I've had a tough life. I was born dirt poor in Texas, and everyone I knew judged me for what I had, not for who I actually was. Given that, I never really had a chance to get very far... My parents were gone a lot, working for peanuts. Dad was always worried about me being ungrateful for being fed. Mom was always trying to keep the peace in the

> household, so I got as far away as I could.
>
> When I got away and started working on used car lots, I found the bosses were always trying to screw the customers, and always trying to screw the workers. Now, since I own my own Lot, I find the City Guys are always out for a Bribe, the lawyers are out for their cut, the customers are trying to get a sweet deal and it's a job just to get my people to show up on time.
>
> So that's my deal, such as it is... What's Holosophy got to give me?

Responsibility - Definition: 1) The Ability to Cause; 2) The Ability to Admit Causing; 3) The Ability to Refrain from Causing.

To be "Responsible" is:

- *To take ownership of one's thoughts, words and deeds.*

- *To choose to see things as they actually are, without shading the story.*

- *To conduct one's life without recourse to blame, outrage, or upset.*

- *To be constantly on the way to a goal of one's own choosing, which may evolve along the way.*

- *To choose to exist or constantly return to **this moment**.*

One cannot exercise that ability if one hides behind an alternate version of the truth, or if one loses track of the moment while arguing a call with the umpire. Responsibility lives in the Now!

The responsible person is present (in the moment) on the

deck, at the wheel, dealing with the wind, the sails, the compass, the ship, the crew and the sky. They are not lost in guilt, blame, or wishing it otherwise. They are right here. Right now. Intending and bringing about a better future!

Others can be found below decks, complaining about accommodation; in the port, blaming the trucker for a late arrival; at the destination, threatening outrage if additional portage is not forthcoming. Meanwhile, the Captain (another word for Responsible...) is on deck, seeing to the voyage and well-being of all those connected.

Responsible people lead their teams, their families, their tribes, their companies and their communities.

Key to being responsible is to make the distinction between the ability to re-spond vs. to re-act. Response relies on thought, estimation, control and decision. Re-action relies on reflex, muscle memory, nerve conduction; but not on thought or consideration.

The responsible party gives thought, takes time, and considers before taking action. A decision is a choice between courses of action. So rather than merely reacting to a situation, the responsible party carefully weighs the options, screens out the urge to react or blame and coolly decides which path to take. One can be responsible and still be wrong or mistaken, but such a person doesn't labor over mistakes or a bad decision, but simply rights things and moves ahead. No guilt. No blame.

So when looking for mates, partners, teammates or friends, seek responsible people; who can leave the sub-rational behind them and continually reach for a higher state of mind.

A Holosopher is known for being responsible for their own condition, and is more interested in what they can create, rather than obsessing about an earlier mistake.

A Higher Standard

"How shall we then, behave? What, about our behavior, defines us as unique? Should there not be a discipline that sets us apart — which defines us as more careful, thoughtful, diligent in caring for and attending to the effect of our behavior on others?

"Shall we demand a free pass to ignore the concerns of mortal beings as we sail on to the port of our choosing? Or, shall we deem that our lives are subject to a higher standard, and conduct ourselves accordingly?"

—Jennifer StJohn

I'm doing pretty well. I've been having some regular breakthroughs in sessions with my Counselor. I've left some old assumptions behind, and I can see the nature of Cognitive Optimization beginning to take shape and reveal itself in my life.

I'm really happy!

I've gotten over some mistakes in the way I've lived my life, and I'm starting to talk with my

> family more often, fewer arguments… It's all good.
>
> But you know what? I've started to notice what foolishness is going on in the world outside of my Holosophy Group. It's crazy out there…
>
> Those people are filled with confusion, upset, drama, crazy emotion, greed…
>
> It's as if all of the worst features of humanity have become visible to me as I started to clear away my own space. Those other people are a mess!
>
> And my partner may be one of the worst offenders!
>
> I catch him/her all the time… Blaming, temperamental, angry, suspicious…
>
> How I ever got connected to that one… Wow! That's a mystery!

You know what? Not everything will be perfect as you begin the voyage of Cognitive Optimization. Sometimes you'll discover that the world has lost its luster, and you're back in the basement again…

Could it be an indication of Sub-Rational thinking that you see everything once again through the lens of criticism and darkness?

So when you (or your mate) "has their head in the bucket," what's the standard of behavior?

What's the protocol when things break down? How should thoughtful people deal with the inevitable moments when it's not polite, not warm — when everything's gone south — when we seem to be taking the Express to the Sub-Rational Basement of Life?

The "Rescue Protocol"

1. Do not react. Pause! Allow a moment of calm to formulate a response, instead.

2. Notice any Sub-Rational Indicators (yours or your counterparts...). Notice, do not read them out in public. Just notice. Allow them to simmer.

3. Do not speak until your comments will be an improvement over silence...

4. Reach for the most compassionate response. Even if it still consists of simple silence.

5. After a modicum of respectful silence, offer up a warm reach... "Hi... I'm your friend Janet." "Your husband, Bob." "Your brother, Tim..."

6. Wait for response...

As things quiet down, and you see each other once again without a Sub-Rational lens, you'll see the reason you fell in love, and the person you were seeing will once again become available — until another mistaken moment.

But over time, such moments become fewer, as your vision and your ability to make rational distinctions become more acute.

Taking a further step...

Wouldn't it make sense, that as an individual began to see themselves, their world and the other people in it more clearly, that such an individual might also become more insightful, more compassionate, more forgiving, and a better shepherd? Consider that seeing the worst in other people might be a habit which is holding itself up for examination... Yes?

The Journey Never Ends

"Do not think that 'enlightenment' is going to make you 'special' - it's not. I meet a lot of people who 'think' that they are enlightened and awake simply because they have had some moving spiritual experience. They wear their enlightenment on their sleeve like a badge of honor. They sit among friends and talk about how awake they are.

The funny thing about enlightenment, when it's authentic, there's no-one to claim it. When you are enlightened the idea of enlightenment is a joke."
—**Adyashanti**

So, I'm very much looking forward to completing my Holosophy studies and moving to Paris to become an author. You know, before I commit to my life work, I want to Establish a Foundation, Get Over the Bridge, Find My Path! Cross the River!

It just makes sense to me to get the heavy personal work done and find myself before I embark on a career doing something else! So, how long will it take for me to finish with Holosophy?

There's an understandable fascination with End Points. Achievement. Arrival. Completion. Getting There! Flying Up! Passing Over!

A man sleeping on a street is "clear." A novice chopping wood is "enlightened," until he starts thinking and gets lost.

We read about Holosophy, and soon begin to fantasize about getting through it, getting it over with, finishing, breaking through!

The Red Fez, The Green Jacket, The Eagle Medal, The Loving Cup, The Auld Mug, The Blue Ribbon, The Silver Bowl, The Gold Medallion...

We do so like our milestones and our symbols of achievement.

We did it! It's over!

Except, it's never really over... is it?

A stranger cuts us off in traffic and we are instantly, reflexively transferred to the depths of the sub-rational cellar, fighting off the urge to joust on the express lanes and destroy this mere upstart mortal who had the temerity to interfere with our Royal Conveyance... Oops. That's one reflex we haven't quite handled...

We're leaving the office late, locking the door behind us and taking the elevator to the parking level. Exiting the elevator, we notice few cars still remain at this hour, and we experience a momentary shiver as our steps echo across the concrete floor. Then we look back and notice a shadow, just appearing by a structural pillar... We break into a jog as we rush to our car, and grab for the keys, hiding in a briefcase recess. Our hand shakes as we fit key into lock and thrust into the safety of the driver's seat, pulling the door closed. Hmm. Guess we haven't completely handled that scenario either.

Sub-Rationality is not a Rational thing, not subject to Logic. It's a Reflex.

So until you actually sit down, pull up a Sub-Rational moment and really confront it, to the point of complete erasure... it retains its place, its anchor, its weight in the Sub-Rational realm. We're not looking for what it means. It's less complex and more powerful than that. It simply kicks in and runs its own unique program.

"Ok. So sit down and relax. Bring to mind a time you encountered this problem... Now, go to the beginning of that incident. Tell me what happened. Play it back for me... right to the end!"

Repeat until you experience a new awareness.

Holosophy is not a "thing" to be "accomplished," or "completed," but a practice which is undertaken to ease the journey of expansion, allowing us to more regularly connect with the infinite.

It's a way of life.

Connections

"Cases don't Make Sense. They Make Connections."
—Jennifer StJohn

Our lives are long. We get input, information and experience from millions of sources under incredibly diverse conditions. Some of those inputs and conditions get twisted around by the circumstances.

Say you trip over a two-by-four in a dark, freezing, wet alley in the middle of a winter night after being awakened and driven out of your building by a fire, narrowly avoiding death! You fall, hit your head on the pavement, momentarily losing consciousness.

How much data is involved?

Harsh awakening from sleep. Chaos. Family. Alley. Apartment. Smoke. Lung Congestion. Fear. Darkness.

Cold. Water on pavement. Two-by-four. Tripping. Losing Balance. Falling. Hitting Pavement. Waking up woozy. Ambulance. Siren. Hospital. Antiseptic. Female Nurse's Touch. Male Doctors' Voices. Gurneys. PA system.

The nature of the problem presents itself. The sheer volume of the storehouse of information available to the Sub-Rational mind is boggling, and worse, it isn't filed according to any Dewey Decimal system for easy reference.

To really penetrate this nest of tendrils, we have to follow one at a time, down through their tangled snarl to the beginning, where we can bear witness to the formative event clearly enough to erase it.

The connections are not subject to our "orders to appear" either. Instead, they are subtle, tinged with emotion, fear, upset or tragedy. The work is delicate and requires patience and a deft touch. As you gather speed and assurance however, the successful case resolution slowly presents itself.

Things Change

"People change and forget to tell each other."
—**Lillian Hellman**

"He who binds to himself a joy
Does the winged life destroy;
But he who kisses the joy as it flies
Lives in eternity's sun rise."
—**William Blake**

"Let go or be dragged!"
—**Zen Proverb**

Ever had that experience? Someone you loved had slowly, imperceptibly changed over time and arrived at a place and a perspective that you hardly recognized? As if there was a stranger in your bed? A burglar in your bedroom? A different person pretending to be your mate, friend, sibling or classmate?

We tend to make a mistake in our approach to life: We look at the people we care about as unchanging, permanent, stable "fixtures" in our universe. We treat people as if they are part of the fixed physical universe — like they have been and always will be "there." This may set us up for some disappointments.

People are not monuments. They grow. They mature and evolve. They Change — sometimes just for the fun of it. People are capricious and subject to their own whims and the effects of nature, time, pressure and happenstance. Things happen. Life happens. None of this is evidence of a hostile force. So you might be over-reacting just a little to the natural process of growth-in-action.

And by the way — it's happening to you as well.

Be warned: everything you think is permanent, may not be... Everything is subject to change, maturation, growth, erosion. Everything. The rope swing in the backyard under the dogwood tree. The boat buoy in the lake. Your brother and sister. Mom and Dad. Your first love. Your best friend, wife, husband, mistress. The coffee shop on 59th street. That old LP record. The car. Your loyalties. The house. Your favorite purse. Your hair. Your politics.

How to cope? Deal with it!

It's all in motion. Beautiful, ugly, sad or majestic;

It's creation at work.

Applications:

1. Personally

Check your assumptions. Has anything changed in the

last decade? Good/Bad? What is driving your decisions in this decade?

2. At Home

Has he changed? Has she evolved? Have you? How about those children? Are they still children? Parents becoming human, frail? Requiring more attention? Do you?

3. At Work

Is there a change in ownership? What about a change in the market, requiring a different strategy? Have the customers found a new favorite? Should your approach mature and evolve along with them? Should you still be working here?

It might help from time to time, to "check in" with your friends, family, colleagues, boss and loved ones. "Who are you today? Here's where I find myself.

Can we find each other and play?"

Everyone changes. It might be nice to tell each other...

Triple Threat

"You can't solve a problem from the same level of thinking
with which it was created."
—Albert Einstein

So, as I read and begin to practice, this reality has begun to take shape: I used to think I. Had. A. Mind. Now I think, I have (or there are) several (dozen) and it's hard to distinguish between them. I've begun to see that there's a lot going on in there that doesn't make any sense.

But even as I understand this, I still find myself doing dumb things. They don't make sense. I know they don't make sense.

But I keep doing them. What gives?

Consider that each frequency of mental activity is a compartmentalized mind of its own, and each is "proof against every other." Each exists behind a firewall, separated and protected from its siblings. Each can independently pretend that there are no others, for each is "proof against its colleagues..."

Sub-Rationality: "Proof against Logic."

The Sub-Rational Realm, with its reflex-dominated operation, doesn't allow for discernment or thoughtful consideration. It doesn't allow for thought.

Any time it encounters something resembling a previous traumatic event, the entire automatic machinery goes into operation — leading to endless derailments of constructive activity. It's not about finding out what's best, but about reacting instantly to "preserve a previous self" from anything perceived as a threat. In that task, it is unreservedly triumphant. But this is a pyrrhic victory at best.

That's why so many people find themselves repeating self-destructive behavior. It seems right and good, not because of its intrinsic value, but because of its resemblance to something that "worked in the past."

To move beyond this barrier, can't one simply "Advance into Rational Thought"? It would seem so, but to really resolve a Sub-Rational barrier, *one must retreat*.

The solution to sub-rationality is to go back to the founding incident and fully erase it through strategic repetitive review: the Transformative Dialogue. With sufficient progress in erasure, the Rational Realm begins to assert itself, perceiving things as they are, evaluating choices, making commitments and following through... The natural cycle of the Rational approach to life.

Rationality: "Proof Against Intuition."

> "Materialism is killing us. I do not mean shopping. I mean the largely unquestioned, largely unconscious, but all-influencing worldview of western civilization that fetishizes measurement at the expense of meaning, objects at the expense of subjects, and more and more data at the expense of wisdom and soul."
> —Jeffrey Kripal

The Rational Mental State erects its own self-preservation barriers as well, tending to view both the Sub-Rational and the Supra-Rational as foreign (and perhaps hostile) states. The Rational individual can make an entire life within the purview of Balance Sheet Analysis. Evaluation, enumeration, give and take, profit and loss, exchange, tit for tat. Entire empires have been constructed with less. Unfortunately, the niceties of beauty, creativity, joy, poetry, inspiration, alliance, the greater good, contemplating the infinite and such are not the purview of the Rational mindset. Consider the challenge of talking about art with an actuary. If you get a discussion at all, it may be a carefully reasoned analysis of the value of a particular piece or artist, but the inspiration that comes from witnessing an item of beauty on display is sadly lacking when the Mentats are in charge.

From the Rational point of view, people wrestling

with Sub-Rational limitations are "not quite human," beneath the notice or concern of the Rationals. The great un-washed haven't the capacity for a thoughtful discussion or a long term plan. And those "Creatives..." No consideration for the profit in it... for analysis. No discipline. Airy Fairy thinking. How can one lay a foundation, build and organize with people who want to sleep late and work out a poem, a musical composition or simply stand and commune with nature? Rationality is a great strength *and* a great barrier to stepping out of the "envelope of self-regard."

Supra-Rationality
Proof Against the Balance Sheet

> "Humanity also needs dreamers, for whom the disinterested development of an enterprise is so captivating that it becomes impossible for them to devote their care to their own material profit. Without doubt, these dreamers do not deserve wealth, because they do not desire it. Even so, a well-organized society should assure to such workers the efficient means of accomplishing their task, in a life freed from material care and freely consecrated to research."
> —Marie Curie

Supra-Rationality tends to be Holistic, Thoughtful, Contemplative, Inclusive, Curious, Creative, Monastic, Intuitive, Musical and Joyful. It also tends to float above much of what ordinary, rational people would deem important, like schedules, budgets, appointments, contracts (as opposed to agreements), and balance sheet productivity.

From the lofty height of the Supra-Rational, the "lower perspectives" tend to appear as needless, joyless, detail-oriented slavery. So much better to step away from acquisitiveness and construction, to get away and commune with nature, the infinite, to experience Satori—the mind-less/self-less connection with all that is.

The Challenge of Communion

> "One sees clearly only with the heart.
> Anything essential is invisible to the eyes."
> —**Antoine de Saint-Exupéry**, *The Little Prince*

Our challenge: to recognize that the human experience is **not** *one experience, but a composite of our experiences across all realms, frequencies and domains of life.*

To penetrate the barriers and history involved in the Construct of the Sub-Rational, we have to overcome the reflex toward "self-preservation," removing the circuitry which keeps us from dealing with life in the moment.

Having removed those barriers, we have to deal with life in the moment and build ourselves the best life possible. The Market beckons.

Having done that, our real challenge as a species is to dream, to transcend our illusory separateness and connect, with each other, with the physical universe and the spiritual—to unify the eight domains and be at home in the infinite.

Proof in Praxis

"In theory, there's no difference between theory and practice.
But in practice there is."
—Anon

Many students are frustrated as they begin their studies. The concepts make sense, seem practical and applicable in life. But after reading an entire book, they still find themselves with fears, doubts and apparently Sub-Rational reflexes in action throughout their days, and lives.

"Why?" they ask, "isn't this working?"

We agree, it is confusing and upsetting. Because to our Rational Minds, "Understanding, Grasping the Concept, Intellectually Capturing the Flag or Getting It", is all that's required. To the Rational Mind, *knowing about, reading about and playing or performing* a Bach Sonata are pretty close to the same thing.

Of course, a few attempts to translate notes on a page into sonic beauty prove that to be wildly untrue! **Praxis is required** — tasting and internalizing the bitter reality of not merely *understanding* but *bringing mastery into being* through repetitive, incremental cycles. **(Conceiving, perceiving, intending, and doing, before actually achieving!)**

The only **handling** for Sub-Rational constructs is to confront them, one instance at a time — working painstakingly through the process. Until, gathering certainty and with increasing velocity you find that you can perceive and directly extinguish sub-rational constructs at will.

Such skill is not acquired by merely reading about it, or *understanding* it, but instead is acquired through personal praxis.

You can *know all about* Holosophy as a rational person, but the Sub Rational realm is just that: Sub-Rational. It is *beneath* Rational handling. It is *pure reflex*. **Proof against mere understanding or intellectual grasp.**

Sub-Rational, Stimulus/Response activity is, in effect "Proof against Logic!" And Logic in turn Provides No Entry into Communion. Communion, also is "Beyond Logic."

So, for this reason, you can't *"**Reason Yourself Up or Out of Sub-Rationality.**"*

Until you sit down, pull up a Sub-Rational moment and really confront it, to the point of complete erasure, it retains its place (its anchor) in the Sub-Rational realm.

You cannot *think or read your way into Supra-Rationality!* You have to *actually go* through the Counseling Process!

Praxis: Summary

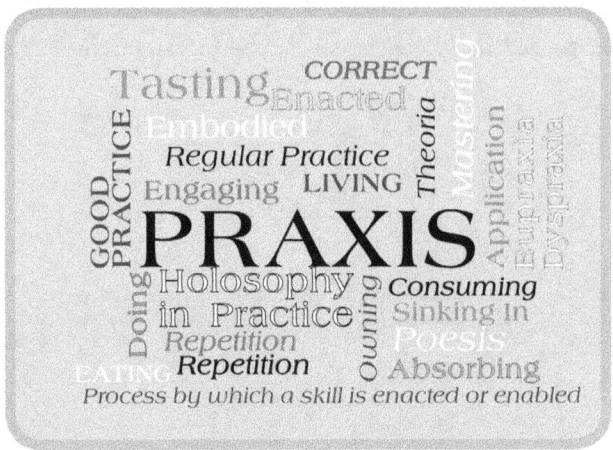

Discovering Holosophy is not the end, it's the beginning of a lifelong study and practice.

The sustained study and practice of Holosophy creates a being who can perceive life (and other people) more clearly, and who will then live more fully, create and experience fewer problems, and serve their communities more successfully.

It's not that the practice of Holosophy adds so much to life, but that it takes away false perceptions, removes inappropriate responses, eliminates hyper-emotional behavior, makes "triggers" vanish, lowers emotional heat, and establishes a firm, rational foundation for day-to-day experience.

A Holosopher is more patient, more forgiving, cooler, quieter, stronger, more aware and less emotionally needy than someone who has not examined their life as carefully.

Our individual histories present a variety of problems,

challenges, learned reflexes, triggers, and perceptions which appear to us as "Character." When challenged though, much of what we think is our "immutable character" is actually revealed as "baggage" and conditioned response. As we look more clearly at our imperfectly perceived life experience, much of it simply falls away — leaving us lighter, more present and more able to deal with what actually Is.

Life As It Is presents challenges, rewards, upsets and confusion. Just as it always has and will. But with Holosophy, we can see it for what it is, without the burden of emotional triggers or historic misconceptions or misjudgment. Life is still full and challenging, but now, perceived accurately, we can play more genuinely and more fully.

Section 5: Then... What?

How Then, Shall I Live?

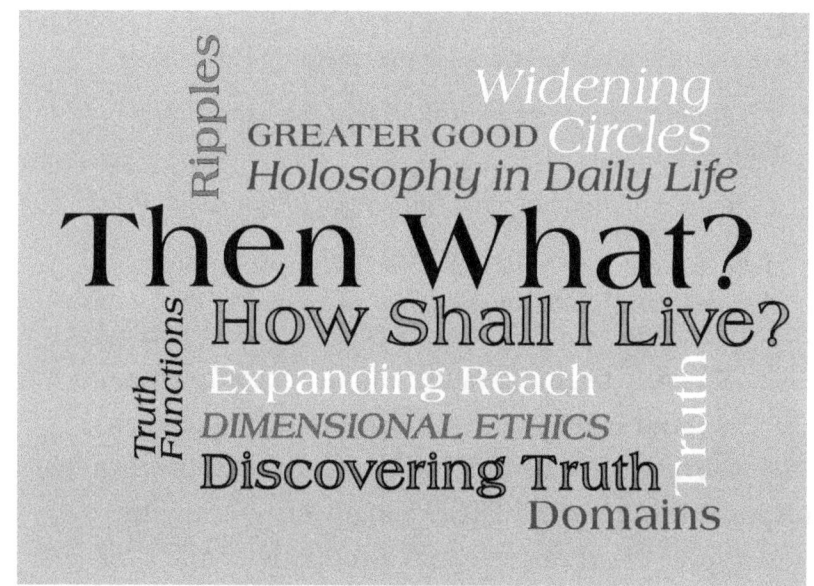

Then... What? Overview

"The issue isn't what to do, but how to decide for yourself!"
—Anon

There are three considerations for the emerging Holosopher:

1. To continue reducing Sub-Rational intrusions into daily life.

2. To expand and enjoy the full scope of Rational ability.

3. To explore, and understand the nature of the Supra-Rational - and lay the foundation of an expanding life.

Having begun (or substantially accomplished) your emergence from the lower frequencies, a new game begins: building a life free of stimulus/response thinking and PTSD Hangovers — moving into a space of greater freedom, productivity and ever-expanding choices. Now that you can concentrate, sustain your attention, and learn, you may wish to exercise that choice across a broader range of endeavor.

First, explore your considerations about what it means to become a more completely ethical human being. Sure, you're good. But what if you expanded your considerations about the "greater good" to include not only other people, but other races, other species, other living things, the physical universe, the spiritual, and the ground of all being? The Kosmos presents itself as your laboratory.

Then there's the question of Truth. What is it? How can you discover it, and benefit from the process? Perhaps a new broader approach encompassing Truth, Ethics and the entire Kosmos can provide you with a suitably fascinating playing field for your life going forward.

Finally, consider that in spite of your considerations that "It's Done! I'm Good!" there may be more to life.

There are some tools required to prevent back-sliding: The Indicators and the Eight Domain model of the Kosmos will, we hope, provide you with the tools needed to expand your considerations about what Lila: "Gods at Play" might really mean for you.

And, should the occasional lost temper, automobile accident or intense counter-intentional moment send you on a deep dive into the cellar, there are some tools to help you re-establish the primacy of reason and compassion.

Home & Holidays

"If you think you're enlightened, spend the holidays with family."
—Alan Watts

Wouldn't it be terrific if we could join our family members at the old home place and enjoy a respite from our burdens? A safe place from the challenges of the world, a group of allies with whom we could connect and grow?

But then comes Aunt Ruby toting her valise of ancient grudges and religious judgements.

Sleek Andrew with his designer briefcase of contempt.

Felicia enters, dragging her scrapbook of familial upsets, each one building on and linked to the one before.

Then Dad, with his favorite discontent, "The Ungrateful Offspring!" There they are, comparing outrages and frustrations, each of them having been set up in life by the old man, none of them evincing quite enough humble thanks or returned support in his old age. Won't they ever grow up, this room full of indignant relatives?

The people we are closest to, are those who know our catalog of complaints. They know our style, our weak spots and our perturbations. Such is the territory of family. At the holiday gathering, there is ample room for jealousy, competition, grudges and critical evaluation to break out in full, angry display.

They see too deeply, they have unjust expectations, and they fail to deliver the required love, respect and tolerance — just when we need it the most. They are family.

So when you think you've got your life knocked, spend some time with them and get a sense of how your policy of forgiveness is working. Check your ability to pause before reacting to another's perspectives. Allow the sarcasm and the judgement to pass by as you yield a position and let the other be heard. This isn't a competition is it? Are love, restraint and support in such short supply?

Or is this reality one that has obscured itself as you pursued your own emergence: they are human, as are we all, and they have traveled a long road to now, with an immense journey still ahead of them.

When you can be the one who wonders at the achievements, offers support for the brave new attempt at greatness, supports the young one, thinking of a first date, re-emphasizes the need for preparation, cuts the carping short and simply hugs the doubtful critic, then... Then you are ready for the next holiday.

But, should you discover that you are still subject to the lost temper, the angry defense of a favorite political player, the resentment of a successful and arrogant sibling, you may be reminded that there is yet more work to do. Then, you must do the work.

There is more than just a single domain to life, we have "buttons" on all of them.

So allow your extended family, your work and the community to continue to push yours and tell you where your next realm of development lies.

Onward!

And try your new awarenesses out on the family next year.

Success in a Small Arena

"A world that truly understands the nature of consciousness
could shift away from the hedonic treadmill of consumerism
and toward the infinitely renewable resource of genuine happiness
that is cultivated by training the mind"
— B. Alan Wallace

> I (We) are doing pretty well with our lives. There's work, family, entertainment, acquisition, competition and well, satisfaction. We've built a great house, and drive wonderful cars. We collect. We're confident about our safety for the future. But I admit, I wonder where the rest, relaxation (and maybe fulfillment) is supposed to fit.

In the Rational realm, one is mostly free of the weight of dark considerations, fears, concerns, anger and depression. Crippling references to History are no longer present. In the substantial absence of Sub-Rational influences, one is able to turn their attention to rational pursuits: Logic, Imagination, Alliances, Trade, Construction... Building a Life.

But, as with so many aspects of life, we're not always so successful as we might have hoped, so our success can sometimes turn out to be the vehicle of our subsequent undoing. As we go further, accumulate more, undertake greater and greater projects, sometimes it becomes obvious that our Rational Undertaking has become both obsessive and destructive — not only to ourselves, but to other life domains as well.

The reasons for this challenge may be found in the fact that our emergence from the Sub-Rational realm is not immediate, complete or all encompassing. With our hard won creative insights, we can clearly see our immediate objective; but we may neglect or forget to consider the effect of our activities on our family, our community, on other living things or the environment. Sometimes we become consumed with our immediate goals and dreams, and lose touch with the larger, greater state of our lives together. Yes, we're making an income, a profit, a positive impact on our community, yet at the same time, we may be creating negative outcomes for those beyond the range of our vision.

Greater Good is aided by a deeper look, a broader vision and a longer time frame.

Without an enlarged, lengthened ethical perspective, we can find ourselves doing beautifully and at the same time feeling inadequate, and unfulfilled.

Because perhaps, we are winning at a smaller-scale game.

We suggest that emergence from the Sub-Rational (Rising from the cellar?) is not done in a complete, comprehensive, all-encompassing way. It is instead, a long-term process of moving up, step-by-step into larger and larger arenas. So while you have stepped away from obsession with the past, you may not have left behind your limited considerations about how far you might one day expand as a human being.

Ask yourself, "What's the definition of a complete life?"

Can you extend even further?

Easily Missed

"Life" is a "Sandwich" of Material Reality and Non-Material Reality or, Something and Nothing.

There's "Stuff" like Money, Rolls Royce Cars, Houses, Food, Rank, Clothes, Rolex Watches... Material Reality. You Know, "Stuff... Things." Nice

But what really makes it worthwhile to have "Stuff?" People might say Love, Respect, Humor, Kindness, Family, Friendship, Learning, Beauty, Service, Satisfaction, Trust, Confidence... Things that aren't Things. No thing.

So, in a perhaps ironic reality, "It is a No Thing that makes Some Thing worthwhile."
—Jennifer StJohn

Hey! I'm winning! What's the problem?

The Daily Program: Start at Starbucks! Then, Outflow! Speak! Hustle! Teach! Meet! Consult! Build! Present! Sell! Work! Repeat!

That's the Winning Formula! At least for most of the culture.

But, Does it feed the Body? Does it feed the Mind? Does it feed the Spirit?

And, which are you?

Lots of what we do feeds the Body. Lots of it feeds the Ego, some of it feeds the Mind. But very little of our daily activity feeds the Spirit.

So we end up expending a lot, consuming a lot — and yet, feeling diminished. Then we try to replenish with food, entertainment, sex, things, stuff, money. And end up, more diminished.

A modest proposal:

We are, primarily — spirit. Of course, it's nice to have a body, and useful to have a mind. But the force, the true resonant aspect of humanity is the spirit — which is without form or mass or weight — and so, easily missed. Ironic isn't it? "The force which through the green stem drives the flower" is the thing which cannot be located or dealt with — except by aesthetics, silence or contemplation.

Seen through that lens, you might better understand why so many well fed, well appointed people seem to be — starving.

Feed yourself. Maybe not first; you have duties of course. But don't let it go too long. Who's going to take care of you? So feed yourself... Every week. Every day. Every month. An adventure. A pleasure. A challenge. Some beauty. Some service. Some love. Touch something. See something. Eat something. Love something, some place, someone.

Love is a very high pitched, delicate and powerful Supra-Rational vibration. Almost ethereal, it feeds, it heals, it sustains, it grows. So get out there and discover what feeds you! And make sure that you're funneling more than enough love, chi, spirit, humor, warmth, consideration, respect and positivity into your universe every day.

Be aware, the most important stuff is easily missed...

Emergence

"Emergence is characterized by longer periods lived in the absence of Sub-Rational indicators."
—Robert Thomas

> So what's it like, living in the World, in a Rational State? How do I behave myself, now that I've got this thing handled?

Out of the cellar, life reveals new dimensions, and becomes an interesting challenge.

There are fewer melt-downs. Less need to "meditate" or back away.

Since you are already calm, you don't need to seek it.

Stress seems less present. You don't get angry so much.

You're not continually "twisted" by events.

In an interesting way, there is a lot less "upset" and there is a lot more centered, smooth, relaxed connection with life.

Maybe you've become less critical, and have relaxed into allowing everything to unfold just as it is.

Simplicity is more fun. That applies to food, people, entertainment, business and community. Complexity is not a challenge, but it's not required for its own sake. Less is becoming, More.

You get more out of your own head, and into the common space. Your thoughts are less about you, your history, your concerns, your needs. You become much more aware of other people, their circumstances and challenges. Your understanding presence is welcomed by people who find you a pleasure to have around.

Your steady silence is interpreted in a variety of ways. Some find you formidable. You say less, and present a smaller target. Some may be threatened. To others, you may disappear, since they are tuned to noise and upset. You may become a source of warmth, support and safety.

You will discover new favorite environments, and may dispense with crowds and confusion.

Look around. It's your world. Make yourself at home.

But watch out. In the center of that satisfaction with your newly found self-confidence, lie the seeds of self-absorbed, self-complimentary, self-absorption. And that's how the Sub-Rational gets re-energized and the entire downward voyage begins again.

The I cannot see itself. So stay focused on what matters, and keep learning and serving.

Growing Circles

"I live my life in growing circles which flow over all things.
I may not achieve the last one, but I will try.
I am circling around God and the ancient tower,
I am circling thousands of years, and do not know yet
if I am a falcon, a storm, or a great song."
—Rainer Maria Rilke

The challenge of any construct or model of life, existence, human interaction or physical reality is that, in the end, it is just that: a construct — an abstraction. We are fond of mistaking our abstractions for traffic lanes and then treating them as physical barriers — mistaking the description for a thing, then believing the thing to be solid. Much later, to our surprise, the entire construct dissolves in a moment of questioning by a teenager with no preconceived ideas.

But, let that not stop us from creating yet another attempt to model, explain, and better understand the way of ethics in life.

Rilke's poem, is an apt metaphor for how the circles of life's multiple domains encompass, interpenetrate and suffuse our daily existence and inform our interactions.

"Life Domains" are not physical barriers but invisible lines of demarcation which help us navigate the shoals and confusion of our increasingly complex interactions within and beyond our individual lives but also between ourselves and the other beings with whom we share the planet, the Kosmos; and the great spiritual force which animates our adventure of existence.

The Eight Domains:

1st Domain: Holon or Individuality - The Self

2nd Domain: Procreativity or The Family

3rd Domain: Community

4th Domain: Humanity

5th Domain: Biology - Living Things

6th Domain: Cosmology - The Physical World

7th Domain: Conceptuality

8th Domain: Infinity

These descriptions are (of course) created lines of demarcation, to make dealing with "the Creation" somewhat less daunting, by segmentation.

We employ the visual image of expanding and interpenetrating spheres as a means of expressing both the universe from an individual's point of view, then the added (infinite) layers of complexity representing everyone, and everything else.

(Our colophon is a multi-colored inter-penetrating symbol of the eight domains of Holosophy.)

Good, in Greater Quantity

"Being Good" is a Great Start! But goodness is more
than the absence of badness.
It's the positive presence and continual creation of
the greatest good.

So I'm good! What's the problem? I haven't killed a soul! Nor have I robbed a bank. I'm paid up in good standing and my accounts balance.

I read to my children, look after my parents, and I'm nice to my wife!

Well, that's Good! Congratulations!

So now, we can freely move into an entirely new and larger area of concern, beyond (and higher) than law or morality. We label this area of study "Ethics" because it considers the ways in which our behavior can not only be good for ourselves and others, but actually be optimized to encompass the greater good encompassing all of life's invisible but significant domains.

Ethics isn't simple. It's not a series of laws or rules, but an attempt to describe existence and the interaction of its various spheres, parts and components and their optimum interaction for the mutual benefit of all — what we have named the "Calculus of Optimization."

So this isn't about sin, or about "banning badness!" It's not about forbidden fruit or about making laws against being mean. Ethics is not negative, it's positive — about making things continually better. And still, Better!

So the dramatic difference in perspective may now have dawned.

True Ethics isn't about not breaking laws, taboos or community standards. It's not about "Not."

True Ethics is a Continuous Positive Contribution to the Greater Good, not only in one's individual sphere, but expanded across all domains.

Ethics is not about shaming or shunning "wrong doers" but about learning from those who inspire greater and greater humble commitment to engineering greater and greater good.

Imagine if everyone on the planet decided to refrain from breathing (in order to cut down on the personal creation of CO^2.) Good right?

Well, perhaps not. They'd have to breathe sooner or later, and CO^2 is what trees breathe. So a "negative ethics" isn't helping.

But what if a great many of us decided to plant a tree, and help others to do the same? Incremental Positive commitment to the greater good. We're in the forest, benefitting from the respite. We're planting trees, getting some activity. We're setting a great example for others and encouraging their participation. Families get excited and make a day of it. Others decide to get involved, and encourage some institutional support. More trees consume more CO_2 which decreases the trapping of atmospheric heat. Green space expands across the planet. Greater and Greater Good across multiple domains.

Shifting away from the mode of "Forbidden Badness," into the mode of "Expanding Goodness" puts the Ethics of the Greater Good into better focus.

Calculus of Optimization

"The Practice of Ethics: The rational contemplation of the fluid equation concerning the optimal outcome for the greatest number of life domains."
—Robert Thomas

Holosophy doesn't promote a Legal or Moral Standard, but an Ethical one. There's no "Code of Expected or Demanded Conduct."

There's no judgement by a jury of perfect people against an impossible standard.

But there is this:

Choose, Argue for and Move steadily toward What's Best for All Concerned.

In Holosophy, choices are arrived at and refined through a "Calculus of Optimization."

What's the optimal solution in this moment, and going

forward, as well as can be discerned, concerning all life domains?

In life, there's what's Legal (or Not).

There's what's Moral (or Not).

Then there is a higher standard entirely:

What's Optimal for all concerned?

It's a big universe, with lots of players, and things are changing — even as we think about them. A "High Ethical Outcome" is a moving target, with a loftier standard constantly presenting itself as circumstances, needs, abilities and realities evolve. If things weren't changing, revolving and shifting in the moment, it might be a less daunting challenge.

Things can always become better, yes? So this isn't about mere judging, but about constantly optimizing — a process that continues to evolve — if only in that as we clear the lens, we can see a more optimum future and embark on bringing it into being.

I Cannot

"The 'I' cannot see itself."
—Jennifer StJohn

"When you recognize that there is a voice in your head that pretends to be you and never stops speaking, you are awakening out of your unconscious identification with the stream of thinking. When you notice that voice, you realize that who you are is not the voice - the thinker - but the one who is aware of it. Knowing yourself as the awareness behind the voice is freedom."
—Eckhart Tolle

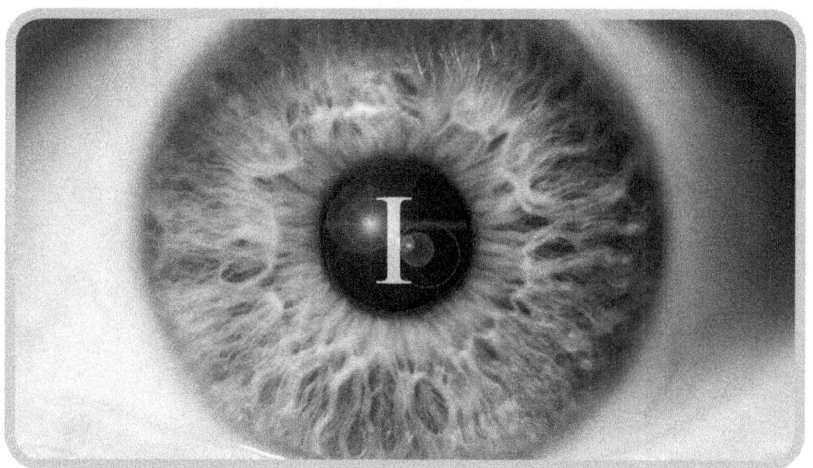

We become so enamored of, so identified with the "viewpoint" we adopt to connect with others in this lifetime, that we sometimes mistake it for ourselves.

Ego, a construct of the Holon, for purposes of becoming visible, for being noticed.

A false "Self." With an "appearance," a "back story," an "important family history," a "great list of accomplishments."

But; being with no wavelength, no location, no physical

appearance, would not worry about how it is "perceived." Though it might leave a lot of happy, evolved self-realized people in its wake.

A lot of "things" and "stuff" fall by the roadside of experience when subjected to the ancient standard of "the Bow of Heaven." Giving to those with little; Accepting from those who have much. Acting without seeking credit. Accomplishing without seeking glory.

Leaving this existence without any monuments, with no obituary. A future much to be desired... and effortlessly achieved.

It may not be that you *achieve* the great outcome, so much as you allow it to occur.

Keep On

"The one thing that matters is the effort. It continues, whereas the end to be attained is but an illusion of the climber, as he fares on and on from crest to crest; and once the goal is reached it has no meaning."
—**Antoine de Saint-Exupéry,** The Wisdom of the Sands

The journey starts with the idea that there may be more to life than merely repairing the damage from the latest melt-down or misestimation. What if life can be more stable, better, even loftier?

Well, it can. And that takes a while; then one gets the idea that there's more to learn, to acquire, to accomplish, to create.

And, at some point, one begins to get the notion that passing along the knowledge might be a meaningful goal as well. So much for 40 years.

It's not as if the journey out of the Sub-Rational, through

the Rational into a more regular existence in the realm of the Supra-Rational can be easily accomplished, or completed in a single lifetime. But it's a journey worth attempting.

The point, after all, is the journey — the adventure and the comradeship and community that might be created along the way.

So start. And keep on.

"'Enlightenment' is not a thing to be sought, nor a state to be achieved, but the process of evolving out of darkness into greater degrees of light. Like the endless cycle of day and night, yang and yin, it is never complete."

Empathy

Sympathy
Your friend is in quicksand...
You dive in under him and push!

Empathy
Your friend is in quicksand...
You find and extend a branch; then pull!

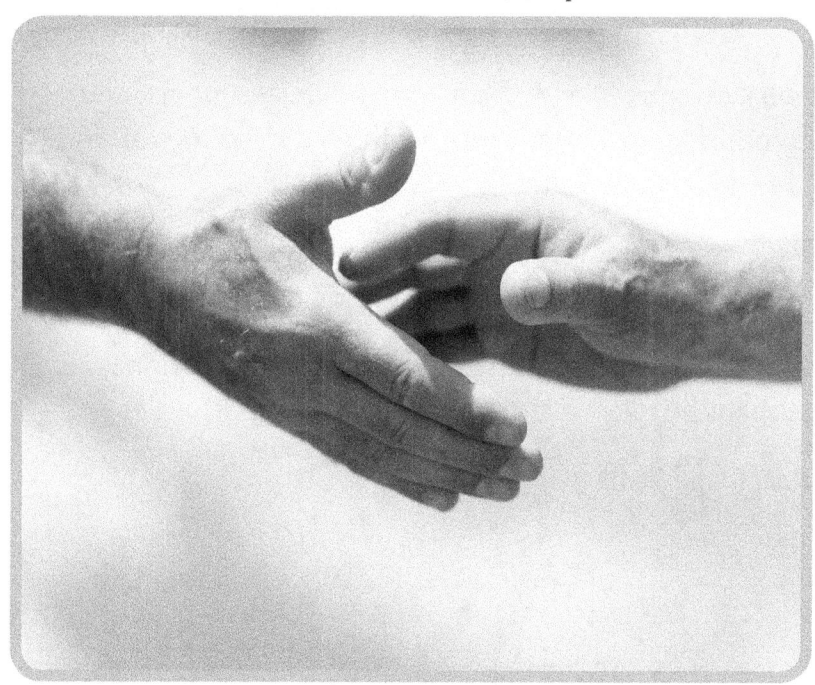

One of the most difficult lessons in Spiritual Evolution, is to learn and practice the distinction between Sympathy and Empathy, or Bearing Witness.

One of your friends has a daughter with a genetic heart valve defect, her days are short, wakeful and painful, followed by nights of more pain and sobbing, periodically assuaged by powerful (and expensive) medication.

What do you do?

Stay up all night in sympathy? Sharing the pain, fear and personal agony? Quit your job and join the family at the bedside, weeping? Perhaps, but this might border on the unseemly.

On the other hand, there is empathy — The ability to reach out and understand what the other is feeling, without the need of experiencing it directly yourself.

You can express helpful concern, interest, support, and commitment without being debilitated in your own work, life and mental health.

Sympathy creates two non-functional individuals or families; both of whom need additional outside help.

Empathy leaves one individual still able to function, and perhaps help.

Reach and Pull!

Commit to Discovery

"The greatest barrier to progress, is entrenched success."
—Anon

So, I've had some wonderful experiences with Holosophy. I've been able to take on some major character issues that appeared at the beginning, to be baked into my personality. As it turns out, they weren't. I've been both surprised at how deep my issues went, and how easily (on reflection) they were confronted and erased.

I've worked through my most significant personal concerns.

I'm back with my family. I'm doing well in my office; nearly run the place now. But as to Holosophy, I feel as if I've come to the "end of the road."

Now that I've got it made, what happens next?

Congratulations! You've moved out of residence in the Sub-Rational realm, and now find yourself with an entire universe in which to make your home. You might conceivably spend the remainder of your natural life exploring the options that the Rational sphere provides.

There are lots of choices:

1. Have a nice life. If something comes up, handle it.

2. Go back and look deeper. Many people find that they still have a case, it's just deeper or more distant from their daily activity — hence, less open to re-stimulation. But that less-examined case may camouflage an as-yet-undiscovered ability in art, music, commerce or philosophy. Have you set your sights too low?

3. Is there more to the Kosmos than self-confidence and success in business, family and community? What about those other domains? How can you help the environment? Other Living Things? The Great Forests? The Aesthetic Realm, or that of the Spirit?

Indicators II

"If the doors of perception were cleansed
every thing would appear to man as it is, Infinite.
For man has closed himself up, till he sees all things
thro' narrow chinks of his cavern."
The Marriage of Heaven and Hell
by William Blake

> From time to time, I lose my temper. Even though I've been doing Holosophy for some time now, I sometimes get the feeling that "bad omens abound." This seems like an indication that all is not as it should be... how should I handle these instances? Does this mean "It didn't work?"

No.

The fact that you noticed something was "out, off or not quite right" suggests that "It" is working just fine! Because instead of wearing those moments of unpleasantness unconsciously, you've noticed them consciously, and begun to question them.

Consider that these moments, days or weeks of temperament, doubt, upset, etc., are indeed "Indicators" of a slip into the Sub-Rational.

So how is life supposed to be? And how do we know when something's not quite right? And then what?

How it's supposed to be:

As you make your way up and out of the Sub-Rational realm, you begin to feel calm, stable, un-ruffled and steady. Not as if it's enforced or required, but there's a steadily increasing presence of equanimity, and a steadily decreasing amount of upset, temperament and stress. Of course, life is still itself — full of challenge, noise and confusion. But now, you handle it differently and better — with greater ease.

How do we know if something's not quite right?

Is there a difference between a stop and a challenge? Between a barrier and a wall? Of course there is. However, when sliding into the Sub-Rational, we tend to perceive things once again, through a darker lens — and then react to the occluded vision, rather than the actual situation. If we perceive unclearly, we act irrationally... QED. Seeing walls and stops, we are unlikely to make progress. So our challenge as we emerge, is to become more and more acutely aware of the character of our perceptions so as to catch ourselves when we slip and "clean the lens."

But maybe you do slip a little, and fall back? It might be helpful to have some clues to provide indications of when things aren't working.

There are two varieties: Behavioral and Perceptual. Herewith, a few examples:

Behavioral Indicators

(With this kind of indicator, we find ourselves obsessively **behaving** badly.)

1. Mis-Emotion
2. Criticalness
3. Continuity
4. Dis-Interest
5. Confusion
6. Dis-Ability
7. Generality
8. Mis-Perception

Perceptual Indicators

(With this kind of indicator, we compulsively *perceive* things in an oppressive light.)

Disengage v. Abandon

Admit v. Commit

Consecutive v. Continuous

Contact v. Intrude

Challenged v. Oppressed

Optimum v. Right

And then what?

There are personal strategies and practices for resolving sub-optimum behavior or perception and enhancing your tenure in the Rational Realm. They can be found in the more detailed books on Theory and Practice listed on the HolosophyFoundation.com website.

Finding Truth

"Once a person is caught by belief in a doctrine, one loses all one's freedom. When one becomes dogmatic, that person believes his or her doctrine is the only truth and that all other doctrines are heresy. Disputes and conflicts all arise from narrow views. They can extend endlessly, wasting precious time, even lead to war. Attachment to views is the greatest impediment to the spiritual path. Bound to narrow views, one becomes so entangled that it is no longer possible to let the door of truth open."
—Thich Nhat Hanh

One of the most dangerous aspects of life is our tendency to adopt a point of view, allow it to evolve into a belief, then close our minds to any other point of view, then move on and start thinking that all other points of view are suspect and deserving of destruction.

We suggest an alternative approach: to support a practice; instead of a viewpoint.

From our perspective, viewpoints are flexible, growing,

evolving tools that human beings use to navigate the shifting landscape of ideas and practices in the world. But if one gets married to a point of view, to their idea of truth, it makes recognizing a better idea rather more than difficult, if not impossible.

What if, instead of adopting a viewpoint, then turning it into an article of faith, we adopt a practice of constantly evaluating and testing the usefulness, the value, the accuracy of an idea or viewpoint? Then, we could submit anything new to a "Test Against the Standard," and reach an unbiased conclusion.

We call that standard, the **Truth Functions.** Outlined in our book, *Holosophy, Discovering the Soul's Code,* the Truth Functions are an ever more precise and lofty set of evaluation criteria against which any idea, statement or practice can be measured.

So, for example, if you've grown up practicing human sacrifice; you could (for purposes of self-development) re-examine your views in a new moment, decide to be "sacrifice agnostic" for purposes of self-discovery, and rate the practice against the Truth Functions and against the Ethics Equation.

Starting from a non-committed viewpoint, using a non-aligned test might give you a sound basis for continuing, or changing your considerations about what is true, workable and, in the end; good. After all, perhaps that person sitting next to you isn't "an offering," but "a colleague."

Truth. Everyone thinks they know it. But few can tell you

why their truth is correct, useful, or from where it comes. Why not examine the Truth Functions and submit your life and its attendant truths to the acid test?

Hold your beliefs up against the standard, and discover how they measure up!

Truth Functions
(How Deep Is Your Truth?)

"I decided to focus on a field where the truth did not depend
on the eloquence of the speaker."
—**Savas Dimopoulos**

"The high-minded man must care more
for the truth than for what people think."
—**Aristotle**

"Isn't looking at the results of a belief
a good way of evaluating whether it's true?"
—**Veronica Roth**
The Divergent Trilogy

We've had just about enough of "Faith." As in, "This runs counter to reason, but membership in our exclusive club requires you to accept all the tenants on "Faith" and to unfailingly practice according to pre-set rules, deferring immediate satisfaction in order to accumulate stature in an unproven after-life... and all of these considerations are not man-made but are, in fact, the ancient Commandments of the Almighty!"

"*We* will dictate the nature of winning and losing, and judge your conduct according to our strict, not-completely transparent rules. Accept now or be denied entry!"

Well, that's what's on offer in the Religious Market, but from the standpoint of the wisdom tradition, there is a wider bazaar of ideas and practices.

Rather than simply state an opinion or conjecture and call it fact, Holosophy proposes to label assumptions and theories as what they are — humble attempts to make sense of the world. We go a little further then, to provide tools one might use to evaluate the usefulness, the application, the value, the truth of an idea, concept or school of thought to see if it deserves a place in daily life and practice.

The basic consideration is this: "How do you know if it's good?" "How do you know if it works?" "How do you know if it's true?" "How do you define Truth, Value, Function?"

These questions are at the center of Holosophy.

We call them the Truth Functions: a set of tools for evaluating the truth, the validity, the usefulness, the value of an idea.

The Truth Functions

1. Is it explanatory? (Do things become clearer in light of this concept?)

2. Is it workable? (Things should work if we rely on them. Yes?)

3. Is it freely available? (Does it come with an Allegiance Test?)

4. Is it rational? (Based on reason or logic... i.e., Does it make sense?)

5. Is it ethical? (Is it good across the domains?)

6. Does it align with or build upon what we know? (Does it derive from or expand a family of wisdom?)

7. Is it indicative or revelatory? (Do we have positive cognitions in its presence?)

8. Does it enlarge us, or take us higher? (Does it suggest a greater, loftier, perspective?)

Applying these measures to a new rule or concept is a great way to evaluate the applicability, functionality, value, depth in essence and the Truth Value of the new idea.

Hell, Heaven, Here

"You can't get to heaven without first leaving hell.
Hell is a Frequency, the Sub-Rational.
Heaven is a Frequency too, the Supra-Rational"

Consider that our life experiences are our own creations, plus what we encounter on the playing field. So, (to employ the old precept) "It's not what life hands you, it's how you respond."

Perhaps the most significant aspect of Rational Life, is that it provides the time, resources and intention required to clear away the ballast and the accretion of the years, and put ourselves in condition to conduct our lives going forward on a loftier plane.

To put it plainly: Here & Now is All. (As far as we can tell.)

We have it within us to grapple with our demons, our collected burdens, and shed them, one at a time. That is a noble undertaking. While we work on ourselves (our great work) we also work at the relationship, the family, the community, the rest of the Universe.

We spend enough time working, and we accumulate a past. We spend enough time clearing away the debris, and we have an insight (or many) and we eventually accumulate a serenity of being. Now.

Enough time spent in serenity, contemplation and continued shedding of excess baggage, and we leave behind all the toys which used to preoccupy our time and space. We enter the Supra-Rational. It's always Now!

Troubles Come With!

"The only ill will you'll find in this valley, is that you bring yourself."
Gandalf, speaking to Thorin Oakenshield...
—J. R. R. Tolkien, *The Hobbit*

I've gotten better at seeing problems coming up, at stepping back when I see things turning darker. Is this the nature of advancing?

To a degree, yes. But the surest way to progress on this journey is to look inward, always inward. It's not them. It's you.

The more we look at that nature of Sub-Rationality, of Success Reluctance, the more we discover that the individual has to step away from blaming or focusing on someone else, and to steadily take individual personal responsibility for their own case, their own Success Reluctance, and for the way they might have (in an earlier moment) misused a skill, an advantage or an ability, and thereby done harm, to themselves or to others.

Of course, this is tough medicine. We might approach Holosophy thinking that we wish to free ourselves from the burden of our past difficulties, and the fears and retrenchment that we've employed to cope with difficult life events.

But the more deeply we look at the circumstances of life, the more we discover that beneath the first layer of an untoward event, lies a deeper level of personal experience where we, as individuals, have encountered a situation where we must confront our own complicity, our own participation in events which turned out unfortunately, or worse, for ourselves or another person. The words "Our Fault" come to mind.

The truth of these circumstances, is that we are very old creatures. We have experienced just about everything imaginable and from every possible position. We have much for which we might and should own up and take responsibility.

In time, as our command of our own history and Holosophy principles expand, we must face the fact that the things we prefer not to think about, are usually things which involve our own misbehavior, our own failure to rise to a loftier standard of behavior. And because we did not confront it **then**, we must, in the end, confront it **now**.

The Game

"All the world's a stage, and all the men and women merely players;
They have their exits and their entrances,
and one man in his time plays many parts."
—**William Shakespeare,** *As You Like It*

I've come to this point having learned to interact with life mainly by imitation and instinct, repeating what seemed to create pleasure, and ceasing what seemed painful. Now that I think about it, that's pretty much "Stimulus Response in a Thimble" isn't it? Is there a more systematic way to approach learning how to live?

Consider that there is a "circularity" about life in that when you push, it tends to come back around, maybe from behind. And there's an aspect of "exchange" as well, in the sense of Give and Take; Push/Pull!

Sometimes it's instantaneous. Sometimes, not so much.

We rely on the Game metaphor to lay a primary foundation of understanding. Life is Play and Playful. Yet many experience life as a darkly ominous, ultimately serious endeavor, which has many life threatening aspects. (Is that an indicator?)

(Of course, any game worth playing would have to be pretty intense, just to keep the interest of a talented player.)

So with that as prologue, here is something to consider as a starting point

Our Hypothesis:

Life is a Game, populated by immortal, spiritual players who assume physical manifestation (with thereby limited life span) in order to enhance the immediacy and apparent importance of play.

The Game has unknown time and physical limits, which each individual discovers and experiences in their own course of play.

The Game has obstacles, challenges, rewards, joys, sorrows and setbacks.

Each player's experience of the game is unique though there are similarities of intention, capabilities, and motivations. Winning and Losing are individually conceived and experienced, according to each individual's Karma and methods of play.

Each player has their own motivations, desires, fears and tolerances.

The players are each playing within a limited set of capabilities to maintain the illusion of limits, stopping points and consensual boundaries. (Physical, Mental, Conceptual…)

The physical "Playing Field" as we know it is the planet Earth, with the greater Cosmos as a backdrop, and the Kosmos — (all domains) as a looming presence.

It began before memory and perhaps beyond our momentarily limited comprehension. It may end, but not soon.

A personal cycle ends after a single incarnation.

Then again, it may recur and continue. And wouldn't that be fascinating?

That Push/Pull aspect suggests that life has an unending "Give and Take" between players, and between and within domains, creating an intriguing level of complexity.

When an experience brings satisfaction, it tends to continue, when it doesn't, it may also continue until confronted.

Get Ready! Play!

What's New?

"Every advance in civilization has been denounced
as unnatural while it was recent."
—Bertrand Russell

"Don't Break My Rice Bowl!" Idiom.
"A new team-mate is enjoined from performing at an exceptional level in order to prevent threatening the compensation scheme of an older, more entrenched player. If the new guy's that good, maybe the old guy has to go..."
—Wikipedia

Well, OK. I'm finding myself pretty confident, and satisfied with life now. I've really settled down, gotten busy on improving my work and my family relations. Things are good! What's to worry about now?

If I get this right, once I've emerged personally, that's it! Maybe I move on and assist others. Is there any other work that I'm missing?

Consider this: "What's Next" is inherently threatening to "What Is!" Entire industries and cultures are built around current facts, ways of thinking and perceiving. With such investment in the "Now," it may be understandable that entire cultures drag their feet on the way to "What's Next."

You've understood Success Reluctance as something personal, somehow connected to a previous painful event, and the inherent fear of new things — the unknown. But think of it differently: as the cultural understanding that anything new is not only different, unusual, perhaps weird; but also a threat — to what already exists. This is not just about your personal circumstances, but about the fact that Success Reluctance is an unnoticed visceral cultural force, operating around the world, in all people and all countries. So conquering internal Success Reluctance and learning your way into emergence is wonderful! AND there is a much larger challenge facing mankind; to evolve our spiritual awareness as a species beyond mere individual, racial or national survival; up to the survival and thriving of all that is.

Without intending to invalidate your individual progress, here are a few indicators of the magnitude of undertaking we encounter as we overcome individual challenges and begin considering larger games.

Medicine:

- Holistic cures for exotic diseases threaten the stranglehold of the pharmaceutical-medical cartel on particular cure modalities. Cancer/Chemo. Diabetes/Insulin.

Transportation

- Electric/Hybrid Engines threaten the pre-eminence of the Internal Combustion/Petroleum model. The Automobile Industry and the Dealers Associations fight back across the board.

- Bicycle Lanes threaten the death grip of the automobile on central cities.

- Cities across the world consider that trash disposal and deliveries would be better undertaken during the night time hours, rather than between Nine and Five. Unions and Delivery Companies respond with strikes.

Employment

- Women Employees threaten to double the labor force (changing the prevailing calculation about individual employee value and scarcity). In previously all-male workplaces, the entry of women sometimes changes the self-perception of the men who came before.

- Robot Employees threaten the "Rice Bowl" of the human workers. Suddenly, there's a "scarcity of work."

Politics/Religion/Science

- *Inherit the Wind*: The "Scopes Trial" puts a high school science teacher on trial for teaching Darwin's Theory of Evolution.

Financial Investments

- The Advent of the Mutual Fund industry and then Computer Trading disrupts the Stock and Bond Brokerage business.

Sports

- Rule changes in Professional Football threaten the stability of pre-existing long-held practices. Two point conversions, no-hit rules on pass rushing.

The Gem Industry

- The advent of "Engineered Diamonds" has been choked off, bought-up and discouraged around the world by the "Natural" Diamond Cartel.

Success Reluctance is not simply a factor in individual lives, but a constant aspect of groups, communities, racial, national even global culture. Wherever human beings are found, there also is Success Reluctance. It is so common as to pass almost completely un-remarked, yet, I believe, it constitutes an existential challenge to our shared future.

Then... What?: Summary

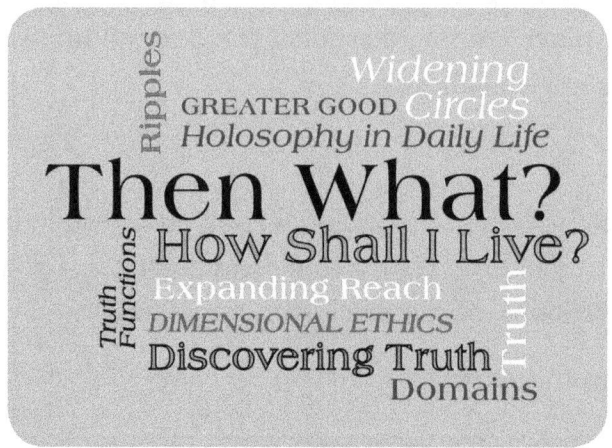

It's not as if one gets "Done" with Holosophy. Instead, one keeps emerging from the Sub-Rational into the Rational and finally, episodically, into the Supra-Rational range of existence. One gains altitude, evolving into their best self. But that continues. That's what we do.

Less Baggage, Loftier Life.

You've learned to look carefully at what life hands you and how you've tended to *react* instead of *responding*. You've begun discarding perceptions and ideas that don't serve you. So keep on. Clear out the closet, the trunks, the attic and the redundant memory banks.

But what happens now? Well, there are no "commandments" necessarily, but there are two tools to assist in decision making: A more muscular perspective about Ethics: "The Calculus of Optimization" and a deeper look at Truth and how it Works — "The Truth Functions."

With these tools firmly in hand, you can see yourself as

more than a mere individual, but also in context as a meaningful part of the great universe:

We are ripples. Life is a Pond.

We are waves. It is the Sea.

You can make a difference, and a good and meaningful one.

Section 6: Commentary

Holosophy In Life

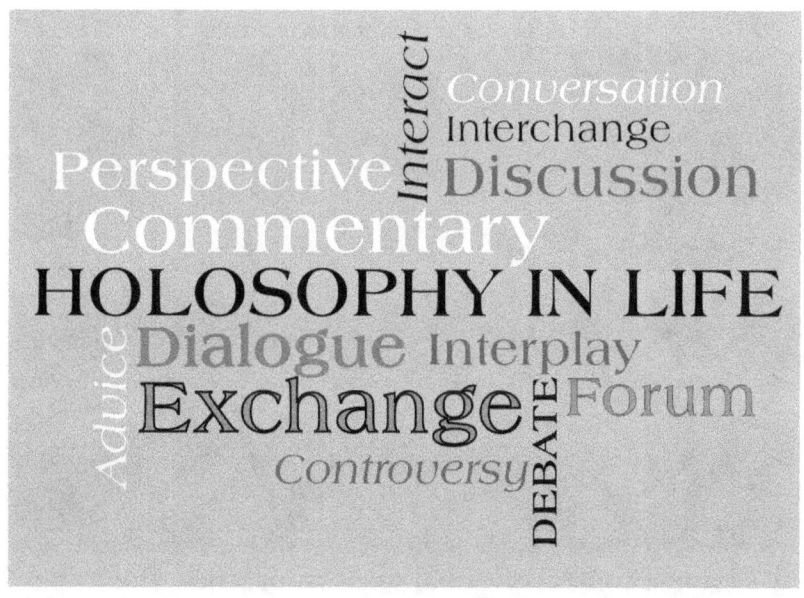

Commentary: Overview

"For centuries, we have been colonized by the idea that the world is mechanic and predetermined and that, if we get to the root of things, if we get down to the basic building blocks, we will be able to control reality. However, the more we go down the rabbit hole, the more things get strange, defying our notions of what reality is. Instead of 'finite and discrete things,' scientists found that *things* change their form and properties in relation to each other, as they respond to each other (and to the scientist observing them).

"We are waking up to a world of relationships rather than things. And what we think of as *things*, are actually intermediate states in a constantly changing network of interactions and relationships. Systems then, are not reducible and predictable; everything depends on the particular and unique relationships which configure and disappear in an on-going ebb and flow."

—**Nuno da Silva**
How to live in a world we don't understand

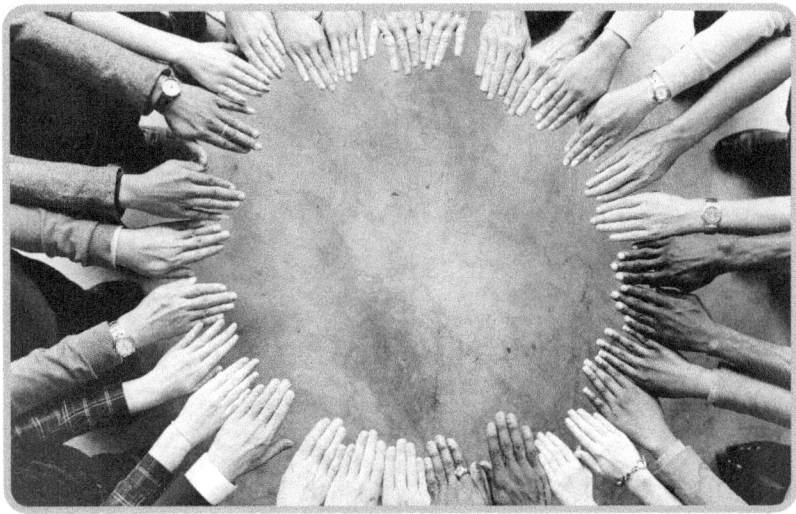

From a context of global spiritual practice, Holosophy is another step on the Great Way. Many of the truths that make Holosophy unusual in Western thinking have been standard practice and perspective for centuries in other countries and cultures: Reincarnation, for example, then Karma, and the irrelevance of "self..."

But while much of the wisdom we espouse is timeless, many of the concepts we introduce will, we hope, take their place alongside the precepts of the Perennial Wisdom, and continue to influence philosophical thinking for a long time to come.

This section presents our thinking on the distinctions between spiritual practice, religion, institutions and belief systems.

We also wrestle here with the daily discussions, challenges and polemics encountered by Holosophers in Life.

Another Turn

"Homo Sapiens is the species that invents symbols in which to invest passion and authority, then forgets that symbols are inventions."
—Joyce Carol Oates

"They did a pretty good job—considering…"
—J. E. Morrow

So, I've done some reading, study and thinking about matters of the spirit. I think Holosophy has some unique things to contribute… But I'm a little nervous about becoming "caught up in a Church."

A little nervous are you? So are we! Don't do that!

Patanjali, Siddhartha Gautama, Lao Tsu, Confucius, Bodhidharma, Jesus, Jung, Freud, Hubbard, Thomas…

Each got it right *at the time* and *in their day*, as well as they could with the tools at hand. Each one moved the hand of the philosophical clock another turn around the dial.

Then human beings — as they tend to do — set aside *practicing* the *teachings*, and began instead to *venerate*, then *worship* the *teachers* — creating **religious institutions**. Each religion created Priesthoods and Dogma, then built Temples, Cathedrals and Tabernacles to shelter the Holy Books, protect the Faithful at Prayers, screen out the "others" and gradually began to impute "evil" to those outside the walls...

Soon, they were fighting to defend *their* teachers and *their* unique descriptions of the infinite, while at the same time to discredit those of the "Others."

And, the cycle repeats itself.

But they did a pretty good job, considering.

A Culture of Enquiry

"Religion is a culture of faith; science is a culture of doubt."
—Richard Feynman

What makes Holosophy so special? Is it considerations about different flavors of mind? Is it an openness to a larger galactic history? What's unique about this study?

We've come a long way, relying first on Religion, then on Science.

But we've reached a point where neither Faith nor Doubt can fully serve our need for improved and enhanced insight and practicality.

We need to move toward a deeper understanding and respect for our physical universe and a more compassionate embrace of our fellows alive together on the planet.

But first, we have to evolve away from our reliance on stimulus/response thinking and get beyond reacting to whatever happens as if everything in the world is a threat to us, our family or our way of life. Not everything is a survival issue. Step away from the weapons. Take a breath, and ask yourself: "Is anything at risk here but your old ways of dealing?"

To grow, we have to step beyond blind faith, beyond caustic doubt or criticality and move into Enquiry. Ask. Search. Experiment. Discover and Grow!

This is not the undertaking of five years, but a lifetime.

Yet, having embarked upon the discipline of inspecting one's thoughts and habits, some fall away for lack of usefulness. Some remain, because they serve an ethical purpose, some are mere artifacts of character.

And, having discarded that which isn't useful, the individual has created space for the new... Skill, Knowledge and most valuable of all, Insight.

False Dichotomy?

"Why does it have to be human or divine?
Maybe human is divine.
Why couldn't Jesus have been a father
and still be capable of all those miracles?"

—Dan Brown
The Da Vinci Code

Male or Female? Prince or Pauper? Up or Down? Positive or Negative? Hard or Soft? Large or Small? New or Old? Current or Out of Date? This or That? Come on, I don't have much time. Make a decision! State your case.

One of the oldest symbols in human existence is the Taijitu: the two in one, the Yin/Yang. Accorded a special place in Taoist Spiritual Practice, in TaiJi, in Chinese Cosmology, and of Pre-Roman Heraldic decoration; the Taijitu suggests that everything in life comes as a matched set of equal and opposite forces.

From a *fixed*, two-dimension perspective, the image suggests a "false dichotomy." (The Yang can never embrace the Yin!) But when seen from a three-dimensional, *active* perspective, the true genius of the image presents itself.

We suggest that our historical reliance on two dimensional "Either/Or" thinking limits our perceptions and our considerations about the symbology of the Yin/Yang... and about life in general! Two dimensional, Either/Or, Goals in Opposition reflect the standard Sub-Rational style of perception.

What if, (as the symbol-in-motion accurately suggests...) life and all of its constituent parts, (ourselves included) are *actually in a constant state of motion and evolution?* What if we are not fixed beings, not locked in place, in character, in location? What if we are on our way to *somewhere else*, to become *someone else*, which will reveal itself as we evolve? If we allow it?

What if life is, in effect, not a fixed, either/or proposition, but a fluid, flexible, ever changing universe in motion, which we can only witness and perhaps embrace as we pass on our mutual paths to somewhere else?

We suggest that a large part of our challenge may lie in the limitations of our historic perception: to our penchant (perhaps internal choice?) for seeing things as fixed, frozen, locked, rooted, stuck. When in fact, everything in life *is in motion*.

This choice, this *habit of fixed perspective* is indicative of the Sub-Rational Range of perception.

When influenced by a Sub-Rational perspective, many believe that *perception is reality, (and that their particular perception reflects a kind of extra special, solid, incontestable reality!)* Don't challenge my assumptions!

We suggest, that **Perception,** *is* **choice!**

Choosing to witness the reality of everything in motion, is a first step toward moving from Sub-Rational, to and through the Rational Range of perception, thought and behavior, and to ultimately take up residence in the Realm of the Supra-Rational.

Belief "Systems"

"Well, 'Religion' comes down to 1-part mystical experience and 9-parts crowd control."
—John Cleese

I find myself hungry for deeper thinking. Something more than sports scores, what passes for politics or finance. But college philosophy lectures didn't do it for me, and being "talked at" on Sundays never made me at home either. So I have a certain reticence about groups and systems and organizations.

Ever felt like singing during a prayer in Church, or laughing out loud, or napping? Well, you're a live human being, and that's exactly what live human beings do.

When we enter a church, or a temple, we are making a tacit agreement to circumscribe our behavior so as to not inconvenience our fellow "worship peers..." But in many cases, our agreements to allow others to meditate peacefully have frozen into the "ponderous burden of solemnity" imposed by many houses of worship.

Can a thing be "stable" without being "fixed or frozen?"

There's a good chance that there's going to be a sunset tomorrow. It will be recognizable as a sunset, but it will be unlike any other.

Be careful your "system of beliefs" does not become, in itself, a prison constructed with bars of frozen thought.

Holosophy practice springs from the idea that *much* of spiritual progress must be made in the discussion between Student and Teacher, or between Counselor and Client.

Anything more "systematic" begins to evoke crowd control.

Previous Station

"In Life, you're a failed prince, a science fiction writer, an unemployed carpenter, or a pretty good football coach who looked the other way. To become Legend, first, you've got to die, then give the elders a little time, funds and a modest tailwind. Oh, and it helps if you can tolerate coming into town on the back of an ass."
—Jennifer StJohn

Whenever I encounter another "New Philosophy," it turns out the founder was some kind of tax cheat, creating a fast buck scheme for self-enrichment...

"… was *nothing but* a Bastard Craftsman."

"… was *nothing but* a Deluded Royal, running from his responsibilities to hide in the forest as a Naked Fakir."

"… was *nothing but* a Hack Science Fiction Writer and Tax Cheat, ashamed of his own first name."

"… was *nothing but* an Unkempt Autistic, who couldn't pass elementary school. When the chips were down, he betrayed the country of his birth and ran away to become the Lackey of the Decadent West, churning out

Holosophy - Conquering Your Fear of Success

>incomprehensible equations."

>"... was *nothing but* a Destitute, Desert Dwelling, Delusional, Misogynist."

>"... *was nothing* but an Egotistical, Half Naked Peacenik, who betrayed the country that gave him an education, and exploited the ignorance and greed of his countrymen."

We say some pretty awful things about those among us who rise up to see further than the rest. When someone sees beyond the lip of the containment, through the bars, over the next hill, beyond the limits of the plateau, through the fictions of the current myth; our cultural guards go on full alert. When a "seer" posits a larger potential, the foundations of our constructs tremble, and the defenses are called up from their rest. Grumpy and outraged, the cultural guardians man their machines of assassination, rotating the rusty turrets to range their weapons on the Prophet in the Distance. And there, the Thinker on the Hill, is revealed against the dawn. A Clear Target for Destruction.

We do nothing so simple as to first comprehend, understand; then argue the logic, truth or workability of premises.

Instead, we disavow his legitimacy as a thinker by demoting him to his previous lowly station. Then we criticize **him** *as he was,* **instead of the idea** *as it is.*

He's not a "philosopher." He has no "credentials." He doesn't "merit our attention." He's a "Nothing but..."

He's nothing but a failed musician. She's nothing but a lab assistant. He was nothing but a college janitor... How could such a lowly creature deserve our attention?

So. It's a strategy for depriving our philosophers of relevance or credibility by focusing not on their greatness, or their contribution; but on their human flaws.

Why should I give any of those frauds my allegiance?

It's a fair question.

But all *great* people, are *still* people.

All great people still eat, sleep and eliminate.

And all of them came from somewhere, began as something, and grew in stature, perspective and insight over time — culminating in an idea, a perspective, a body of work, a contribution — which might actually deserve to be engaged fully, directly, without reservation, in the full intention to discover its benefits, accuracy and efficacy in resolving our current difficulties.

But great people threaten our safe, established myths and explanations, so they must be brought low; and quickly! There is no tool so effective as reducing one to their previous station, and then annihilating that station.

The moral? Don't discount someone's wisdom because of their lowly origins. You may be right about where they came from, how they were raised, or what they did. But none of that takes away from the relative truth or applicability of **their ideas. Engage the ideas, the teaching.**

Leave the teacher and their previous station out of the equation.

Not Required

"When people are fanatically dedicated to political or religious faiths or any
other kind of dogmas or goals, it's always because
these dogmas or goals are in doubt."
—Robert M. Pirsig

So what's required to study, practice or connect to Holosophy? After all the press about cults, fanatical followers and charismatic teachers, I'm not only defensive, I'm downright suspicious!

Holosophy is merely a set of facts, premises, statements, suppositions and calculated assumptions about life and our part in it. It is primarily concerned with what we would call the Life of the Spirit, and Spiritual Discipline.

Faith is not required. It doesn't require defending. Testing however, is absolutely essential.

What is required, is a sustained interest in pursuing the assumptions, mistaken beliefs, momentary failures to look, and the sometimes willing suspensions of disbelief that are required to make family and community life possible — or at least, less unpleasant.

As you discover more and more about how you've gone about creating your own life, and about how you can independently, and more perfectly *re-create* it, you'll find that less and less in life requires *faith* in something unseen, unproven and unbelievable.

Life itself is a limitless parade of miraculous occurrences. But the more of these you encounter (or create), the less you'll consider that they have to be "externally sourced."

And then, the fun begins!

Hucksters

"It's called 'Spiritual Discipline' because, like any discipline, it requires regular and dedicated practice. Not over 24 hours, not over a weekend, not for an hour in the bookstore, but over a lifetime."
—Jennifer StJohn

"Hey. I just came back from a weekend workshop on Spiritual Power! Wow! What a blast! We didn't sleep for 24 hours. I am so blasted and sacred! My whole being-ness is elevated and clean."

There seems to be a market for Hucksters selling Spiritual Insight in small, crunchy (but very expensive) bites. Imagine the blatant un-reality of a group of workmen erecting a "native sweat lodge" in the parking lot of a hotel in preparation for a 48-hour Spiritual Weekend of Power!

It lays out so clearly our consideration that great wisdom is hard to obtain, therefore it must be good if it's expensive. (Or perhaps, it must be expensive if it's really good!) In reality, price is rarely an indicator. What is more likely is that the work will be demanding of your will, your time, your narrowly allotted commitment — and to some degree, your resources.

But what makes it, (and you) "Good" is the degree to which you master and continually apply the teachings and the technique. Beyond an amount which indicates a fair exchange for the time and the prior study and dedication; price is irrelevant.

A genuine teacher will not be arguing prices or "deals" with you. More likely, the higher practitioner will ignore you or insult your dedication and be through with you.

If you're hungry in spirit and seek to improve, find someone who's spent a lifetime in study, ask them quietly about what they've lived and learned and enquire as to their willingness to teach you — then shut up and pay what they ask. Arrive early. Stay late. Clean the study area. Bring tea. Honor your commitments. And enjoy the passage of years as you too, experience and grow into Mastery.

Move Toward Beauty

"The basic recurring theme in Hindu Mythology is the creation of the world by the self-sacrifice of God. (Sacrifice meaning, "to make sacred.") God becomes the world, which, in the end, becomes again, God. This creative activity of the divine is called Lila — the Play of God."
—Fritjof Capra, *The Tao of Physics*

A Hierarchy of Effects

Some effects are really classy — even Elegant! Like Gift Giving, Healing, Teaching, Supporting a Family, Caressing a Child, Dancing, Writing a Play, Cooking Dinner for a few hundred patrons, Rebuilding after a Hurricane, Tranquility and Beauty, Commitment, Designing a Tablet Computer, a Barn Raising, Humor, Conducting a Symphony — Performing a Score that you've personally composed. Curing Cancer. Running a Business. Training a Thoroughbred. Creation.

Some Effects are not so high flown: Slavery. Nasty Temperament. Meanness. Cruelty. Addiction. Stupidity.

Sitting in front of the tube for a century or two... An epidemic of Malaria, Floods in old European Towns which collapse everything in sight, ruining historic spaces as well as killing the inhabitants. Rage. Natural Disasters. Cancer. Theft. Rape. Murder. War. Destruction. Death of a loved one. Suffering.

There's a difference between things that happen, things we make happen and things that happen to us. Some are higher flown, and some are less lofty. Some are welcome. Some are not. If you had the time, you might rank-order everything in creation by how lofty, how welcome, how creative and how positive its effects, results and outcomes. (Or how negative.) You might then decide where on the scale you choose to operate: creating outcomes or merely experiencing them.

Pick Your Flavor

Is it possible that part of life is choosing what you'll be about, and what kind of creations and effects you wish to bring to the arena? What if life is not unlike a great shop-counter, where you can survey the available life choices, decide upon which one (or many) you prefer to create, and resolve to dedicate your life to bringing that about? Your Choice! Once? Or many times? Grand, or Granular? Big performance in front of the entire world? Or an intimate demonstration of grace for a few disciples? Up to you! Create or experience, or both...

Another approach might be to experience things, as in a Game.

In a game, the players define the nature of play and participation, choose up sides, pick positions, practice, play (perform/compete), argue about calls, enjoy or rue the results, and resolve to come back better next year — or stalk off in a huff. Maybe the team didn't choose you: How to respond? All of those are results/effects — and each of them can be compared to all the others. Some players we love, some we despise — (same with teams, universities and countries) all based on the relative quality of the effects they create and allow us to experience. So it's not only about what you experience as a player, but also about what everyone else experiences. Better? or Worse? Is it a Benevolent effect? Or Malevolent? Does it make you and others happy? Or not?

Maybe life is more like a game than we thought.

In looking at it, there are lots of things happening — some beautiful, some not so much. There's the matter of chance of course, but also how we all choose to react and carry on. It's not that everything is pretty or perfect, but that through our own efforts we may be able to bring about "a finite increment of betterment" (a small but meaningful improvement).

We can "optimize" things to create better effects. And we can optimize the way we respond to what comes our way.

Consider that Life may have a purpose. It might be more than vast chaos.

It may be an infinite, endless game and you may be a Divine Player:

A God at play…

Well?

Start where you are; Play! And "Move Toward Beauty."

Bearing Witness

"A thought transfixed me: for the first time in my life I saw the truth as it is set into song by so many poets, proclaimed as the final wisdom by so many thinkers. The truth - that love is the ultimate and the highest goal to which Man can aspire. Then I grasped the meaning of the greatest secret that human poetry and human thought and belief have to impart: The salvation of Man is through love and in love."
—**Victor Frankl,** *Man's Search for Meaning*

A person I know recently walked away from friends, family and the shared experiences of the last fifteen years and became a violent, abusive drug addict. I couldn't influence him, couldn't get through, noticed that whenever I said anything, it was as if he could hear the sound of the words, but couldn't comprehend what they meant. He was so married to his new path, that he could not see what was happening, didn't care that his sheer existence was threatened. And, inevitably, he died, alone and uncared for in the most awful way.

Doesn't Holosophy provide tools for being a positive influence in situations like this?

When people "shock us," it may be because we've assumed something about them, and are then brought up short against actual reality: We thought them to be A or B or C. And what they actually are is X or Y in this moment, and on their way to Z at some future time. Our assumptions about other people are exactly that — our assumptions.

Not that our perceptions, expectations and opinions are without weight. On the contrary, our ability to influence others is powerful and can be of great benefit in helping people find their way in a tumultuous universe. Life and literature are full of examples of people or groups that have totally changed or at least influenced the trajectory of someone else's life. But our impact may not be enough to totally change that life path that lies before another. At day's end, it's their choice: Accept your advice and align with your intention? Or set another course?

Then again, perhaps their purpose had something to do with changing us.

Tough. You may want the best for your friend, and be saddened when they go another direction. Maybe you saw them inaccurately, as something you hoped they might be or become. Maybe they were never that person, or just not capable of becoming.

Maybe they just decided to go another way. Maybe you were wrong about the nature of "best."

The most challenging part of living on a planet with seven billion people is that each of them has a unique point of view and a different perspective about what's "best"

— which may change in the next moment. You may be perceiving it accurately, or not. You may disagree about both paths and outcomes.

But the initial and most intense challenge is to see that individual as they are at this precise moment. Now! What about Now? In this exact moment, who and where is that other person? Where and what will they become? It's their future to own — and yours to witness and perhaps influence.

Just realize that while they're not beyond your reach, they are indeed beyond your control.

The concept of "Bearing Witness," relates to this delicate line in human affairs: to see what is happening; to take notice; to comment; to hold your position with empathy and commitment to what's best; but to stop precisely at that grey area between where it is strictly yours and clearly theirs.

Spanning that distance is the work of love.

Would that we could reach out and put people right back on the path where they belong! Yet, that pretty much defines the limits of one person's reach. You can help. You can try. You can make the attempt. In the end you can love.

The Perfect Tool

"To a man with a solution, everything in life looks like a problem!"
"To a man with a hammer, everything in life looks like a nail!"

More than a few times, I've encountered people who have found "The Answer" and just can't wait to sell it to me, get me to join the club or commit to a monthly shipment of "The Perfect Solution." Are you hiding a case of the stuff in your closet, just waiting for a weak moment to sell me something?

TaiJi

I've spent a lifetime working this art and practicing whenever and wherever I find time and space. I've traveled the world accumulating information, experience and connections relating to my art... I'm really good at TaiJi. I might actually be a Master. Writing better, negotiating a real estate deal, healing a broken bone, all of these can be resolved with the proper application of Chi!

or... **Christianity**

The perfect answer to everything. And because I have devoted so much time and effort to mastering my religious practice, I feel that it is the answer to every challenge that life throws at me... Weight loss, social anxiety, public speaking, navigating a foreign city — all can be addressed and handled through prayer and the divine intercession of Jesus, the Christ.

or... **Holosophy**

Well, don't even start. Holosophy can help you see more clearly, become more genuinely yourself, navigate the landscape with greater equanimity, and become a better-rounded human being. But it still won't help you dress for a date, cook dinner or balance your accounts. You still need to live, to experience, to expand your boundaries. (Ahh, that's what Holosophy is for.) Don't lay all of your life's ambitions at Holosophy's door.

But the whole point of this deal is to be a Human Being. Right?

So **do** your Holosophy, but then go **be** Human and **have** a perfectly wonderful life!

Go study painting, history, cooking, business... Live! And live better, understand better and be a better friend, parent, teacher, lover because you understand life more deeply. With less and less baggage, **you** become the perfect tool!

Into the Mystic
Intimations of the Infinite

"We're already in the presence of God. What's absent, is the awareness."
—Richard Rohr

"Silence is difficult and arduous, it is not to be played with. It isn't something that you can experience by reading a book, or by listening to a talk, or by sitting together, or by retiring into a wood or a monastery. I am afraid none of these things will bring about this silence. This silence demands intense psychological work. You have to be burningly aware of your snobbishness, aware of your fears, your anxieties, your sense of guilt. And when you die to all that, then out of that dying comes the beauty of silence."
—Jiddu Krishnamurti

So what's it like to progress to the upper levels?

From time to time, if we remove the spiritual underbrush, and give sufficient room to our transcendent nature, the universe gives us a flash of insight. A momentary ascendancy to the Supra-Rational. No, you can't live entirely in that realm and remain human, but deep practice seems to decrease the distance between, and increase the frequency of peak experiences.

.....

That perfect afternoon, driving home with the top down, into the sunset. A single beam of light seems to stretch out directly from the sun itself, with singular focus which guides you back to the dawn of creation...

At that moment you realize time is mutable and this moment is forever.

.....

You've experienced an injury. In the cramped hospital room, there's no place for that vase of fall flowers. A maintenance worker enters the room with a mop and notices the flowers on the floor, nearly squashed in the corner. She moves on, silently, but soon she is back with a table and the flowers find their rightful place in a wash of afternoon sunlight. You discover that not all healers wear white coats.

.....

Of an afternoon, you're perched on a rocky outcropping near the summit. It's sunny and warm. The climb has been challenging but not a deadly risk. You decide THIS is the perfect spot for lunch. Pack laid aside, you reach for the food bag and remove sliced meat, crumbly cheese, nuts, crusty bread, and a pastry, then the flask makes its appearance. With each bite, you find yourself drawn more powerfully into the beguiling reality of food, taste, sense, joy and one-ness. This is *not* a picnic. It is the food of the Gods. Your taste buds expand and the world recedes but for the view of forever off to the south.

Is this heaven? Death? A moment of perfection? No matter. For if it all ends now, what more perfect moment could possibly appear?

.....

That dark night, Hospice... Mom, recumbent and nearly invisible in the mechanism: part bed, part morphine injection system, part patient manipulation crane... The beeping of the heart monitor sets a steady and excruciating rhythm as the moments drip from the hourglass. Taking a break, walking the endless hallway, you become aware of the intimate and overpowering Presence of Death. Seeking a momentary respite, you enter the adjacent room. Penetrating the gloom, you see a middle aged man, standing near the bed, holding the cold hand of an aged woman. You say, "My mom is next door," he nods. Standing silently together, you are sentries against infinity. Eventually, you touch his shoulder, then embrace him quietly. He accepts in silent communion.

You quietly leave and return to your lonely station, standing guard. Time passes. Your wife arrives, joining the vigil. You sense movement, and turn, to witness the man from next door, joining you. Together, the three of you bear witness. He eventually reaches out, and bestows a hug before silently departing.

We are allies. Death has no dominion here.

.....

One doesn't simply "finish with mere mortality and rise up." But instead, one studies, practices, and incrementally removes the accumulated weight of lifetimes. As you steadily discard more and more baggage, you find less holding you down, and you can freely turn your attention to work, play, family, education, ecology, community, philosophy as a welcome and productive member or leader of the community.

As your practice matures, you leave more and more behind, simply being present in the moment. Without noticing it, your presence matures into a more fulsome, mature gravitas. That foundation paves the way for one, many, or a steadily appearing series of divine moments of connection.

The Supra-Rational is with us and in us always.

Our challenge is to stop finding reasons to build barriers to insight, then to reach out through our practice to find, first, a degree of clarity and stability, then to embark on the long voyage into the Mystic.

Degree of Emergence

"I saw an Angel in the marble, and I carved until I set him free."
—Michelangelo

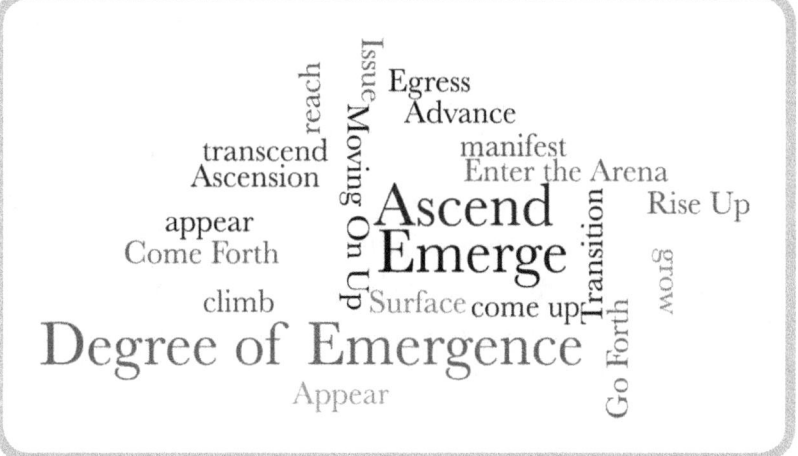

Am I done? I've looked hard at my case. I've forsworn Sub-Rational Indicators. (I've got the list on my refrigerator door) I notice and re-set almost instantly when something caves me in momentarily...) I've been working not only on my own case, but on expanding my purview beyond the first domain to the second, third and so on... I'm beginning to get a really broad-minded perspective about ethics and the larger universe! So is there a Map? Where do I stand? Is there a great catalog of attainments? Are there Merit Badges? How about a Medal? I'm on the verge of Godliness, right?

Well, perhaps not...

Gods are not busily keeping score as to their own degree of personal emergence. They are not comparing. Gods are creating and manipulating Universes. They are exterior-focused and creating miracles. So when you find someone with an Ego, busily "measuring their mastery", they are definitively not there yet!

And if that's you we're talking about; well, there may be a distance to go…

While we're on the subject, consider that the reason you're here, may have something to do with joyfully engaging the challenges that life presents. You're not here to leave the game, but to continually learn how to play not only more effectively, but more joyfully, effortlessly and beautifully; and then to teach others.

So, it's a matter of degree… The speed with which you rebound after a setback, the confidence with which you handle hostile people, the certainty that you now manifest when causing a challenge to vanish. The urge to "mark your spot" or "measure your growth" against the yardstick of life is powerful, but perhaps indicative of an "as yet to fully mature" perspective.

We are each unique, and given to distinct paths and abilities, beyond simple comparisons. Why not measure yourself against the universe, and your ability to confront and hold your position against the life domains: one at a time? It's a challenge to confront, meaning to hold one's position and one's character against the countering powers in the family, the public sphere, the international order, other living things, the environment, the cosmos, aesthetics and the infinite…In short, the all-inclusive Kosmos? Now that would demonstrate a significant Degree of Emergence!

Isn't this why you're here: not to gather applause or acolytes, but to blissfully live, learn, make progress and maybe shed some light on the path for those who follow after?

The most evolved people are not those with the big houses, the private jets, or the most fans. Evolved people are those who leave others glowing in their wake with a plan for continuing their own emergence.

And **this** is the Game; not the mere acquisition of things or certifications, not the leaving of it, or defeating others, but continuing to carve as you set yourself (and others) free.

One, Two, Three!
"What ought we be?"

"That is the essential question,
the question that concerns spirit and not intelligence.
For spirit impregnates intelligence with the creation that is to come forth.
And later, intelligence is brought to the bed of creation."
—**Antoine de Saint-Exupéry**, *Flight to Arras*

First, you work on reducing your time in the sub-rational cellar. You become aware of the fact that you know in a deep way that there is more to life than settling old scores, or resenting how your parents treated you. You long for the opportunity to just set a goal, and then go about achieving it. That pleasure in seeing things clearly, then demonstrating what intellect, study, work and commitment can bring about is beyond price. But building (as fulfilling as it is) is a limited undertaking, with a circumscribed beginning, middle and end.

But that's not the end of the journey — for it is a journey.

We are an old species. We have experienced and accumulated untold trauma over uncountable years. Getting clear of the multitude of historic incidents (on every domain) may be the work of a lifetime. But as you remove the detritus of history, and satisfy the need to accumulate and build, you begin to feel the pull of a larger, more substantial life undertaking. You begin the work of continuously expanding access to the Kosmos through and across all domains, gathering insight, clarity and perception as you go.

So what are the steps? What else is there?

1. Reduce Sub-Rationality through Cognitive Optimization using the Transformative Dialogue.

2. Maximize Rational Understanding and Functioning... Increasing both Ability and Productivity.

3. Discover Multi-Dimensional Ethics and the Truth Functions.

4. Continue study, engage in Tutorial to reveal the Kosmos in its multi-domained glory, and begin to conceive of and experience increasing familiarity with the Supra-Rational.

5. Live there, enjoying flashes of insight, joy and satisfaction.

6. Then repeat the process, teaching others the way.

Imagine…

The Hidden Good

"It's one thing to see the obvious bad in the world.
Quite another to discover (or become) the hidden good."
—Robert Thomas

"The things we admire in men, kindness and generosity, openness, honesty,
understanding and feeling are the concomitants of failure in our system.
And those traits we detest, sharpness, greed, acquisitiveness, meanness,
egotism and self-interest are the traits of success. And while men admire the
quality of the first they love the produce of the second."
—John Steinbeck

Perhaps we've stepped through the looking glass, entering a world precisely opposite of that which we truly desire.

Honesty is on the ropes. Integrity has taken a break. Self-dealing is the norm in consulting. Bankers use **your** money to finance estates and art collections attesting to **their** "taste." Lawyers seem to take your part, but while you consider the middle ground, they inflate the conflict — and their fees. Men of the spirit seem dedicated to putting the "Gospel of Success" in God's Mouth, while benefiting from your largesse.

It may not be the world we hoped for. So... What? Be good anyway!

May we suggest, that you put aside what's going on out there, and decide on your own what you will make of your piece of it? Making something wonderful in spite of the times in this arena, now that would be a victory!

- Small acts of Selfless Service.
- A Force for Good.
- Random Acts of Kindness.
- An Underground of Lofty Aspiration.
- An Army of Compassionate Listeners.

Identify your favorite contribution and start in - the world will follow!

One You

"No man, for any considerable period, can wear one face to himself and another to the multitude, without finally getting bewildered as to which may be true."
—**Nathaniel Hawthorne**

There's a great discussion of the last thirty years about creating "balance" between one's personal life and one's professional undertakings. Or of balancing work and play. As if the components of life are somehow to be seen as "in opposition to each other." Of course, in the 50s there was no need for balance or compartmentalization, because men "worked" and women stayed home. Because women also got the kids, the compartmentalization was automatic! It didn't work all that well — else, Why the Revolution? But it was a system.

Then came the 60's and the revolution and the desire to Have it all!

Then the compulsion to Have it all! Then the insanity that ensues when attempting to Have it all; then the rush to retire to have just a little part of it all. Then the resignation to never actually having had it all.

So much for the last sixty years.

We're noticing that many people are having trouble dealing with the challenge of being everything and everywhere, indulging in everything, to do (and excel at) everything!

While the opportunities are everywhere, we should perhaps not feel obliged to launch into all of them simultaneously. The elders have been telling us forever, "You can't be two places at the same time. You cannot be all things to all people."

You cannot have everything. Not all at once!

Life — is — choice!

Wow! And what a life we've been having! At this point, We're prepared to suggest that the attempt at Being, Doing and Having it all! may be a fool's errand. And Keeping it "Balanced?" Right! In your dreams!

Yet, many of us allow our mind to rush around, thinking of everything, evaluating this, criticizing that, finding ourselves inadequate, hoping for better, fearing the worst, insisting on spinning and spinning and spinning — and missing that fact that the entire universe is right here, right now, ripe for the taking. We try to be stable in the office, and also to be a party animal, then an obedient child, and perhaps a financial gambler. All these collected "selves" pulling in different directions at the same time — leaving us stranded in the center — feeling pulled apart. And we find ourselves one morning — seeing the two (or many) faces in the mirror — and not knowing which is genuine. The very definition of an existential crisis.

> "How can you be two places at the same time, when you're really nowhere at all?"
> —The Firesign Theater

So, pursue your dreams; but allow us to suggest a simple approach to staying sane in the attempt: Stick to a single you. At Home. With the Family. At Work. In the Community. In the silence of the great forest and with your dog.

Some existential instructions:

BE! Not be this, or that, or anything else... Not something you mistakenly label as "Yourself." Simply Be! Don't "talk." Don't "think." Don't "act."

Just Be!

Now, Choose what you wish to DO. One thing only. Make tea. Brush your hair. Write an article. Dress. Eat. Drive. Greet. Sit. Phone. But not all at once. And try to do whatever is in front of you with the full commitment of your Body, your Mind and your Spirit. All together.

Then, Have. Have the moment. Have breakfast. Have the feeling of your new shirt against your skin. Have the grief of losing a loved one. Have the tranquility of breakfast by the lake — or at Starbucks.

The simple truth of this life is that we cannot Be anywhere

but Here.

We cannot Do anything but what we're doing.

We cannot Have anything but what we're having — at this moment. Though life has a variety of domains, and we may play in any or all of them, the challenge is to bring our authentic self to each.

One life, and a single self, presenting a single face to all constituents.

The ultimate test of a character choice, is whether it will play with equal effect, in one's own mind, at home with the family, at the office, in the community, in the nation, in the silence of the great wilderness and with one's dog.

Be. Do. Have. One at a time.

Buddha would approve. So would Lao Tsu, Yeshua, and Confucius.

*Presented with Love and affection for **Baba Ram Dass**; teacher and author of "Be Here Now!"*

Wider Perspective

"For those who believe, no explanation is necessary; for those who do not believe, no explanation will suffice."
—Michio Kaku

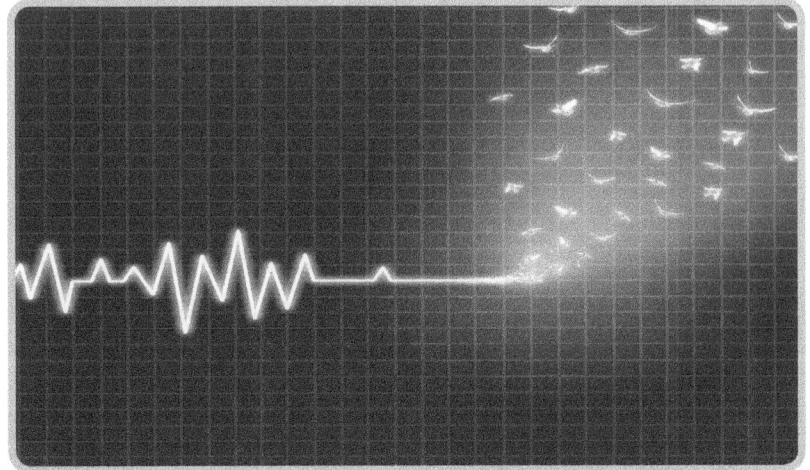

After four decades and 2500 cases, the researchers at the University of Virginia have reached a conclusion: "Reincarnation is Real!"

To the satisfaction of the scientific method, reincarnation is fact.

(Pause for the obligatory resort to searching, finding and reading the appropriate materials.)

Are you back?

Well, that certainly enlarges the realm of discussion, doesn't it?

What happens after death? Well, now we know at least a little better, with a more scientific and somewhat factual underpinning.

For centuries, reincarnation of the spirit has been understood to be a reality by a large portion of humankind. Others have subscribed to differing theories — often with a messianic fervor. But in few cases have people taken to heart the key lesson: "That what you create in this life cycle, may be exactly what you find yourself born into in the next!"

But now, we live in an age when research, myth and poetry come more significantly into alignment.

Now... Wouldn't you like to leave this world better than you found it?

What, Again?

"Much of existence is a reactive and repetitive function of our many lives."
—Jennifer StJohn

All right, I've been reading about the "previous lifetime" literature, and I'm not all that interested in discovering whether I was King in 1253. So what's the point of all the discussion about past lives. Isn't this just gossip — albeit on a grander scale? Suppose it's all true. It strikes me as nothing more than an endless series of dull, repetitive smallness.

You died horrifically, in a basement room, in the dark, tortured by a rotating group of evil ghouls. It was seemingly endless, and pointless. For you had nothing to give, no secrets to reveal.

Then, earlier, you died an anonymous death of a

bullet wound on a battlefield, alone, cold, in pain and without solace.

Then there was that exploding, ugly demise on the battleship during a sea battle — cannon fodder, indeed! Reduced to food for fish.

And those were just three.

What's the take-away?

Death is often pointless, meaningless, without justice, reducing an individual to — mere elements.

But then, a larger awareness: that one's life can generate and manifest value, protect people, enlarge the game for everyone. That a single individual can create meaning. And that this single series of realizations demonstrates that "life" is indeed an endless, recurring miracle; the meaning of which is to be found (created actually), not only in an instant, but in the sheer infinite number of ways it might be experienced, re-experienced, and ultimately ennobled. But, not until the mundane is understood in minute detail, fully confronted and finally, transcended.

At the first level, an awareness (and a hovering burden of sadness) that death can be pointless, meaningless and utterly without a lofty aspect.

But underneath and within that, the lofty truth that life can be, and is — holy.

Inside the curse, a truly beautiful blessing.

For an engaging literary exploration of re-incarnation, enjoy **Groundhog Day.**

Birthing Our Future

"Our lives are not our own. We are bound to others, past and present, and, by each crime and every kindness, we birth our future."
—David Stephen Mitchell, *Cloud Atlas*

> Ok, I get that I'm at the wheel of my life here. It's a big responsibility. But I can take it! I'm up to the challenge. After all, it's just 70 years over and out right? What's the big deal?

A Story

If you are in a rush to get through the monthly tasks, and hurry to the insurance office to secure next year's coverage, you might be forgiven for being somewhat curt and a little inattentive.

But then, the Agent, who also is in such a state, remembers and won't greet you with excess warmth when you come to him next month for new coverage on your vintage sports car — which requires an over-the-top level of attention to the details of model year, state of repair and previous damage, if any. So he drags his feet, pays little attention to the details and issues you a policy that is more expensive than required and fails to deliver the added coverage for expected wear on the suspension, shocks, brakes and those very expensive tires.

You're a busy person. When you take the car to the dealer, you haven't time to hang around to converse with the specialist about maintenance, so you rush away with your rental car, saying, "Just handle all the maintenance as specified in the insurance package... it's all in there!"

Of course, it isn't. So he handles only what's covered, and makes no comment.

You return later, after he's gone, to retrieve your car.

That evening, your son, with a great deal of pride, borrows the classic for a big date with that special girl — your boss's daughter. The sporty classic takes the curves with élan, and the date goes beautifully — until the ride home. Showing off a little, your son pushes it while taking the big curve. Well, the unmaintained shocks react badly, the brakes fail, and the car skids in the curve, down the cliff and onto the rocks. Both children are killed. The authorities rule it "mechanical failure." The adjustor has a different word for it — Negligence.

Your job? Well, that's a memory, and the trial begins next month.

It's your "responsibility." That doesn't mean that you are bad, or wholly to blame; but that you influenced what happened to you and the others in your life and that you can influence what happens next.

You can claim to be a victim of circumstance or other people's lack of due care. Or you can cease blaming, stand up and begin to realize that your conduct has had, and will have outcomes. Whether you like them or not, they arise from your behavior and actions. With each decision, you foreclose or expand your future range of opportunity. Today is the Mother of Tomorrow.

Going forward, you again have the opportunity to influence what happens next. With each action in each arena; you may build a constantly growing sphere of influence from which you can birth not only your own future, but thousands of others as well.

Dessert:

Cloud Atlas is a movie with Tom Hanks and Halle Berry. Under-reviewed because of its complexity, it is not easy, but is entertaining and engaging far beyond mere entertainment. It opens a window on the discussion of how our daily behavior may indeed be part of an ongoing pattern of repeating lives. Take a long evening, real friends, food and wine enough to see you through the experience and the discussion. Enjoy!

Fundamental Non-Local

"The fear of total annihilation at death has caused more human suffering than all physical disease. If consciousness is both fundamental and nonlocal, we can make the case for immortality of the soul."
—Dr. Larry Dossey

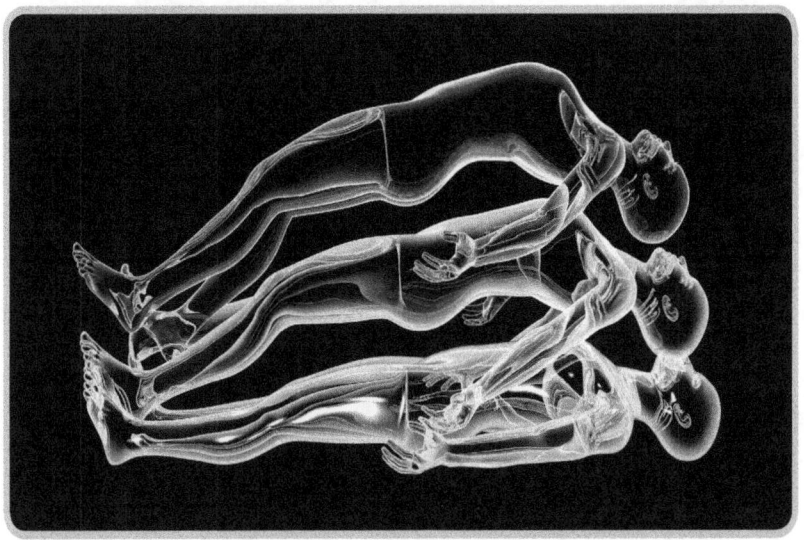

Well. That's sort of the elephant in the room, isn't it? We're prepared to countenance serial reincarnation as a fundamental part of life.

Our own experiences confirm this as a natural fact.

Many of the elder cultures on the planet already consider serial life experience to be a reality. As more and more evidence presents itself, it becomes more and more difficult to deny the fact that "life" may actually encompass many lives!

Quantum Entanglement (or non-locality) at a distance would suggest that "The Force" is not a physical thing, hence it can and does animate without presence.

So the combination Body, Mind, Spirit might easily replicate itself from body to body and lifetime to lifetime. But this is simply theory.

Explore your own case and see what appears. You may be surprised, and then, expanded. How bad can that be?

Or maybe a "just to be safe" perspective is in order. Why not build your bridges, buildings and life in such a way that you and your children's children in a subsequent life can cross that river with confidence? Apparently, ethics and reincarnation can go hand in hand — whether there's "proof" in this moment — or not.

Maybe

"We choose our next world through what we learn in this one. Learn nothing, and the next world is the same as this one, all the same limitations and lead weights to overcome."
—**Richard Bach,** *Jonathan Livingston Seagull*

It's seventy years (or so) and out! That's the terrible burden our primary assumptions about life place on us. But what if, maybe, we're mistaken?

It's already proven that reincarnation is a convincing reality. (See UVA Study/Reincarnation)

So now what?

What if we are always passing this way again!? Working our way once more around until we learn all the lessons, play all the games, accumulate all the experiences and decide to rest for a while as teachers/helpers?

Could we improve things? Can we perhaps, improve our ability to navigate the between-lives path with greater dexterity, and so, come back with ever-enhanced net ability? Could we better the life experience of other races and living things? Could we improve the health of our planetary home, or even make it possible to expand into other galaxies? Could we conceive of loftier games?

Why not? Give it a try!

One's Own Truth

"And now the end is near
And so I face the final curtain
My friend, I'll say it clear
I'll state my case, of which I'm certain
I've lived a life that's full
I've traveled each and every highway
And more, much more than this
I did it my way."
—Frank Sinatra

Nothing is quite so dear, quite so clear, or so deeply valued, as one's *own* truth.

We each encounter life *from* our own perspective, *through* our own unique viewpoint.

And, we draw conclusions — about the nature of *what* life is, *how* it is to be lived and *how* to win or lose — from our own experiences.

We play. We lose. We win. And we emerge — with an evolved perspective.

Nothing in life is so sacred as one's own conclusions, one's own thought processes and one's own viewpoint. How can one be anything but absolutely in one's own mind?

But what if one is finding that somehow, something isn't quite functioning? What if the conclusions seem to be "off" just a little bit? Could there be a mistake in the workings?

How many people are happy to go back and check their learning, their assumptions, their founding life premises, and their hard fought conclusions? Few things are so sacred.

The fundamental understanding in Holosophy is that life is long, and each of us has had a stressful moment or two, in which we reached conclusions or made assumptions about something, which we continue to desperately grasp for years, decades, even lifetimes — because they are "**our own truths...**"

But the fundamental willingness to *question everything* — **especially what one holds dear**, may be the most important aspect of the successful personality. If the external reality is not to your liking, check out the internal reality — and prepare to revise and rethink your own truths…

Chop Wood. Carry Water!

Perhaps everyone has heard or read the story of the Initiate asking the Zen Master, "Tell me of Enlightenment!"

And once the story rolls easily off your consciousness, you'll have time to consider the story and its meanings more deeply.

Chopping wood... We all know what that means. But do we, really?

Have we considered that identifying, clearing, felling, sectioning, splitting, barking, preparing, chopping, carrying and stowing wood (before reducing and removing the stump), might fit under the heading of "Chopping Wood?"

Have we considered that finding a dipping point, carrying buckets, reaching into the stream, circling the bucket, drawing it back at the right moment, dipping the second bucket, hoisting the pair, walking back home, emptying, then stowing the buckets, then putting the water to use, might all comprise "Carrying Water?"

All that is involved in the simple phrase, "Chop Wood. Carry Water!"

Every Day.

For a Lifetime.

That's the "Practice of Enlightenment." The incremental nature of coming into your own true character through the steady removal of false selves, ingrained assumptions, forgotten but absorbed crises and assumed burdens. It doesn't occur all at once, but in thousands of large and small revelations... the steady accumulation of grace and wisdom.

When all that's done, (Is it ever done?) well, you've got people to teach. Chop, chop!

There's Time

"There is neither spirit nor matter in the world;
the stuff of the universe is spirit-matter.
No other substance but this could produce the human molecule."
—Pierre Teilhard de Chardin

Consider the possibilities…

Ancient civilizations, flung across the galaxies in multitudinous volume.

Intelligences in mind-boggling variety, engaged in projects at levels of sophistication which make our greatest works seem childlike.

And of course, these beings and their planetary cultures, may have known about us far longer than we have even conceived of them. (See Best Answer page 131.)

What if a new level of game begins as you read this?

What can we create now that we know it doesn't stop with a single person, or a single lifetime?

What if we have… time?

Spiritual, Obviously!

"The Ignorant are fanatically religious.
The Intelligent are fashionably atheist.
The Wise are obviously spiritual."
—Pandit (Maestro) Ravi Shankar

There's a war on, between the "Reductionists" who suggest that there is no spiritual component to life; and the "Holistic Thinkers" who consider that life is a composite of the Physical, Mental and Spiritual.

To put it bluntly, there are those who think man is merely material, not possessed of an independent mind, free will or, soul.

Then, the contrasting view that the human being is a composite — a Spiritual Being who manifests mind and free will through his primary possession, a physical body.

Two points of view in a deadly competition.

It's a war. The consequences beyond calculation.

Have you decided where you stand? Which side you're on?

With sufficient personal experience, the debate may appear moot to you.

But such disputes have a way of becoming intense, personal, immediate. Be sure you know where you stand.

> Life is a mystery. You cannot understand it unless you surrender,
> for your intellect cannot grasp its expansive and infinite nature,
> its real meaning and fullness. Bow down low and humble;
> then you will know life's meaning.
> —**Amma**

See: Holosophy — the Best Answer page 131.

The Long Road

"It's a long, long road, from which there is no return.
While we're on the way to there, why not share?"
For I know, He will never let me down...
He ain't heavy. He's my brother!
So on we go."
—Bobby Scott & Bob Russell

Start with one domain, the First. Work on it. Handle that horrible moment when your bike crashed on the big hill.

Then that time when the rope broke over the swimming hole.

There was that time you fell down, went to the hospital, the darkness and pain.

So handle them! Then handle your persistent self-sense of victimhood.

Vaporize it.

Handle that college break-up, and the string preceding it. Handle Betrayal. Handle that divorce. Then work through the family judgement thing and never feeling confident about Dad's love. Then those empty, lonely solo holidays.

Work it back through all the previous losses in their bewildering volume.

Move on. Damaged by politics. But now, getting the woof and warp of the great tides of history and how immense groups of people have behaved.

Begin to confront the endless lifetimes involved, and the galactic histories.

One step at a time, you become more solid, more at ease, more certain of yourself, your intentions and your abilities. And you've begun to expand your connection to the deep Kosmos. Your insight has deepened and widened, and your ability to acquire, influence and control your own life and those of others is expanding dramatically.

Domains: First, Second, Third, Fourth, Fifth, Sixth, Seventh and Eighth.

It's a long, long road…

Puzzles

Holmes: Learning to see the puzzle in everything. They're everywhere. Once you start looking, it's impossible to stop. It just so happens that people, with all the deceits and illusions that inform everything they do, tend to be the most fascinating puzzles of all. Of course, they don't always appreciate being seen as such.

Watson: Seems like a lonely way to live.
Holmes: As I said. Has its costs.
—Robert Doherty, *Elementary*

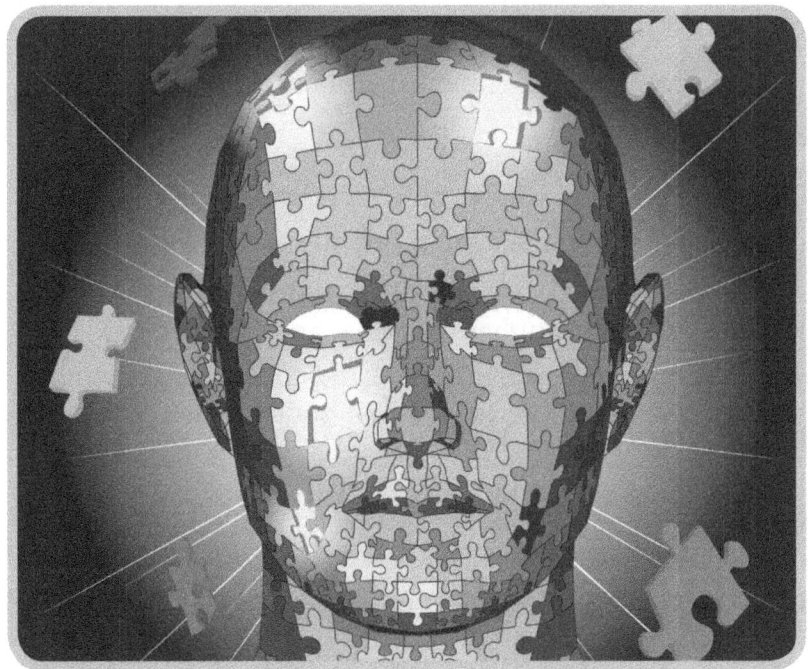

As your practice evolves, you begin to notice the games-within-games being played by people all around you — those you love, and everyone else.

Our lives are complex, layered, personal, the results of ancient commitments and confusions making contact with and interacting in impossibly sophisticated ways with everyone we meet. There is no simple explanation for why we instantly dislike this person. There is no one set of instructions for dismantling the animus we feel radiating from that individual we've only just met.

And though it would seem simple to help that individual see their way through the holidays, it is indeed, anything but simple.

Your mother arrived at the doorstep of your life by an impossible path. Your father sired you as a simple action, a small part of his ancient, layered existence. You have come to this very moment as part of a series of unique interactions, some of them purposeful, some random... as have we all.

But, if it were simple, we'd have a handle on it — wouldn't we?

Instead, we have only the thread which terminates between our fingertips. So, pull gently, and confront what is just within reach. Assimilate that lesson, and move forward.

Commentary: Summary

We expect that Holosophy will go forward, become accepted, grow and become another part of the Perennial Philosophy.

And.

Examining the fate of other great teachings gave us pause.

People and societies tend to make predictable misjudgements in how they care for belief and practice systems that become part of global culture.

They tend to lionize or disparage the teacher(s). We suggest that **the teachings are important, not the individuals who brought them into the light.**

The studies, beliefs, practices take on added stature as they gain acceptance. Things become solemn, agreed upon, humorless, dark and deep. Priests and Officials emerge. Collections are levied. Statues are constructed, columns are erected, great books are printed with gilded pages. The thrust of the once-active personal study gradually recedes into groupthink.

Don't let this happen.

Keep Looking. Keep Catching Yourself. Keep Laughing.

Section 7: End

Your Turn

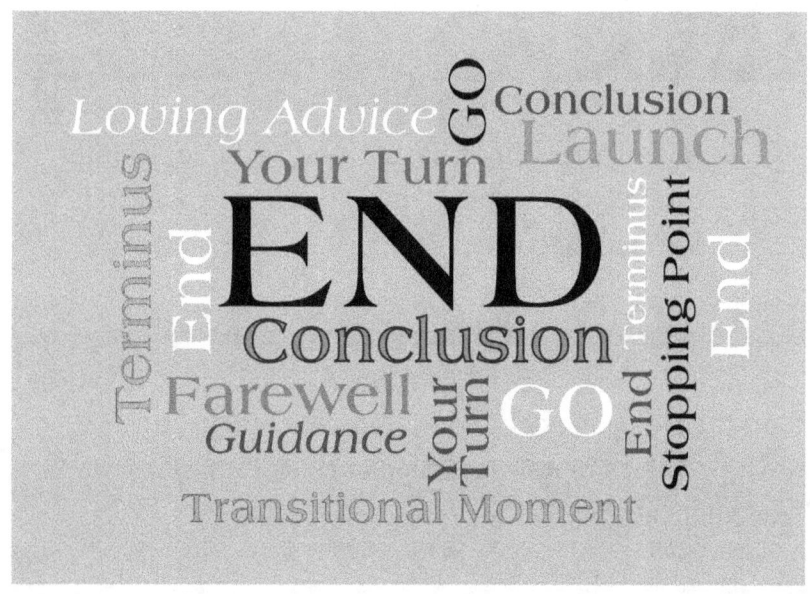

End: Overview

"I slept and I dreamt that life is joy.
I awoke and saw that life was service.
I acted and beheld, service was joy."
—Rabindranath Tagore

British Museum Reading Room

You've gotten a look at this now, and it looks interesting… (Or it doesn't, in which case; Farewell, move along!)

But if it does look interesting, why not act now!?

Find the Holosophy Foundation online and keep the link. Check in now and then and see if there are new publications.

Pick up the next book in the series and make a list of questions.

Invite someone else to read, too. You're going to need a partner…

Start a Discussion Group!

And don't be a stranger. It's a pleasure to travel with friends…

What remains in this chapter is a matter of fond farewells and thoughts about the future of this young undertaking and your future if you choose to become a Holosopher.

Defending Our Delusions

"One of the saddest lessons of history is this: If we've been bamboozled long enough, we tend to reject any evidence of the bamboozle. We're no longer interested in finding out the truth. The bamboozle has captured us. It's simply too painful to acknowledge, even to ourselves, that we've been taken. Once you give a charlatan power over you, you almost never get it back."

—**Carl Sagan**

Consider that to create the game of life, there had to be (at some point) a consensus agreement to pretend unknowingness.

Then, we have to agree to learn and know more, but only a little bit at a time.

Then imagine someone comes along and threatens to remove your illusions!

Well, you're going to resist that with every fiber of your being.

That's the nature of Success Reluctance.

So, if you find yourself, at some point, defending your delusions or limitations… **Stop!**

Holosophy's Character

"The highest forms of understanding we can achieve are laughter and human compassion."
—Richard Feynman

"Keep me away from the wisdom which does not cry, the philosophy which does not laugh, and the greatness which does not bow before children."
—Khalil Gibran

"There are two kinds of light — the glow that illuminates, and the glare that obscures."
—James Thurber

Laughter is the greatest indicator of upset resolved, occlusion dissolved and wisdom discovered. Laughter dissolves barriers between people, nations, parties, points of view and the worst barrier of all — that which comes between us and the truth.

Laughter. Something to be prized as an indicator that

we have dissolved a false belief, a misunderstanding, an ancient self-perspective — or an untruth.

If there is laughter, there is possibility, forgiveness, the death of ego and the emergence of a greater potential.

It's about time for a philosophy which can lighten the room and our burdens... Make room for the glow and warmth of laughter!

No "Robe" Required

"Wisdom does not wear a robe, a watch, or a badge of rank...
Do not conflate *wisdom* with *a* teacher, or *any* teacher."
—Jennifer StJohn

So, do I have to "Buy a Robe???"

You're not going to start dictating dogma, reciting catechism, or demanding that I believe or buy something, are you???

I've been through the religious/philosophical wringer with my family, community and church over the fact that I found much of their program simply unbelievable. Not only that, I discovered that when I had doubts, I was treated like a leper and pressured to buy in, go along and shut up.

So, I'm skeptical...

Am I expected to join something, bow my head, and get in line?

In a word, No.

Holosophy is a perspective about the nature of life, a collection of philosophical writings (some would say wisdom...), a set of spiritual practices, and a body of collected experiences and discussions in the form of those who practice...

It is not a club. Not a church.

The Holosophy Foundation was established in order to publish the works of the authors to benefit individuals seeking to improve their lives and expand their philosophical understanding.

No "Robe" required.

Altitude

"Let me take you higher, softer, clearer, better, kinder... Let me guide you home."
— Anonymous

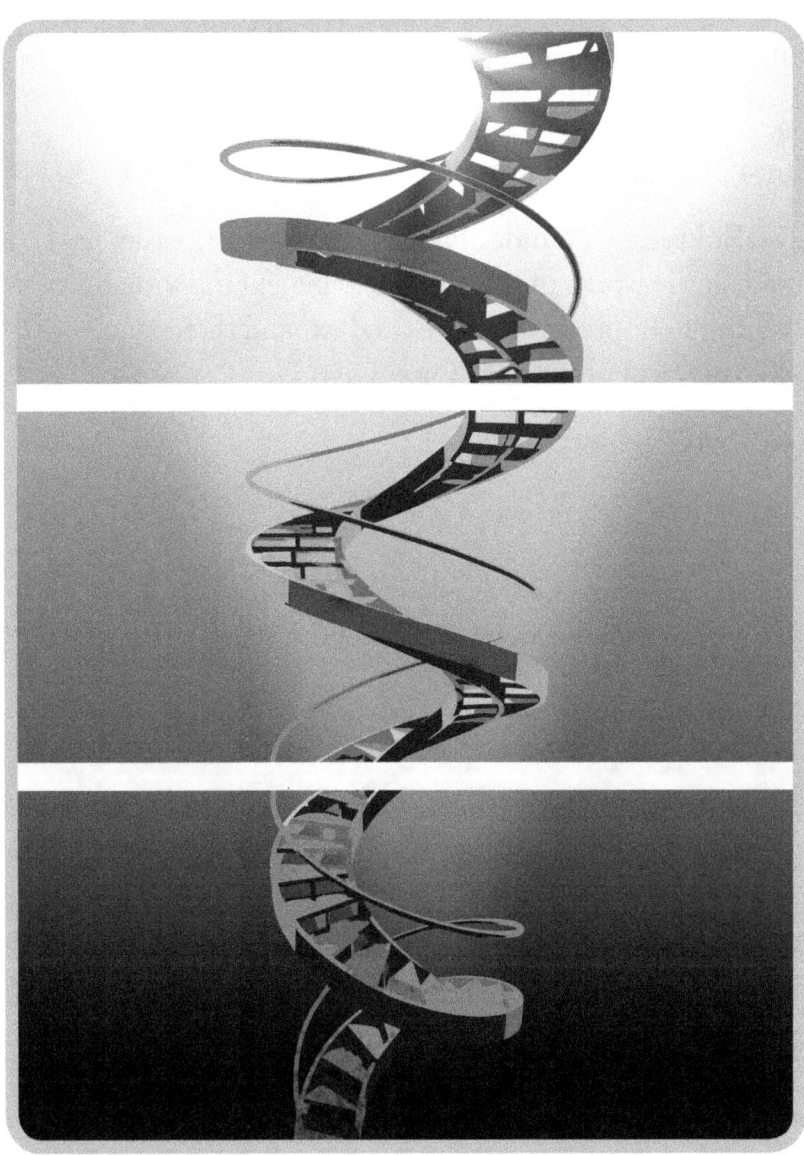

In the end, it's about Altitude. Whether you have room in your spiritual cloakroom for discussion of Karma, Reincarnation, the Relative Age of Humankind in the Kosmos, or just about how to survive a Holiday Season with the relatives; it's about Altitude.

Have you succumbed to recurrent replays of distant, ancient upsets? Are you merely existing; low on the scale? We call that Sub-Rational.

Or have you succeeded in putting most of that drama behind you, much of the time? Are you building something? Focused on the details!

Bravo. You're in the Rational Realm.

Have you come to a balance in your life? Have you enough? Are you moving higher toward a goal, with some accomplishments yet to be discovered as you go? Are you of help in your family, in your community, in your work? Do you have the occasional occurrence of grace? Humility? Joy? Consilience?

Congratulations... Welcome to Supra-Rationality.

The journey from lower to higher frequency, from lower to higher altitude, is that of a lifetime, and consists of many advances and temporary retreats along the way. May the road rise to meet you! May the wind be always at your back!

Not the Teacher

"One does not have to be an angel
to be a saint."
—Albert Schweitzer

People approach the Perennial Wisdom, often by looking for a guide. They search for a suitable teacher — a person of upright character, thoughtful demeanor, kind affect, a piercing intellect, and a loving disposition. Having found a suitable candidate, they sit back and wait for the dispensation of wisdom — which they may, or may not espouse or act upon. Then they proceed to bring up the "wisdom" in a friendly discussion with another seeker, comparing the characteristics of their teacher with those of "the other guy."

What ensues is a merciless comparison of the "teacher features," between seekers who are not practicing what was taught, but are instead, looking for someone to "follow" who can withstand the criticism of all comers.

"My teacher's bigger and better than your teacher! My teacher is beyond reproach!" If I can besmirch your teacher's character, then his teachings are suspect by association! And I'm pretty suspicious of your teacher — there's something oddly off-putting about his look, sound, attitude, hygiene, perspective on football, etc.

But what if it's not about the teacher — but the teachings; and you?

What are you doing with what you've learned? Have you let it touch you — change your perspective, your way of thinking, your behavior, the way you treat your family, house, dog, colleagues? Your teacher may be a genius — or not. He may be an upstanding individual and good at math and music. She might be a terrible dancer. That's not the issue. She might drive too fast... But it's not about the teacher...

It's about, and it's up to — you! What will you make of what you know? What are you doing with what's been taught? How are you using your knowledge to help yourself and others? Are you applying it? Or just collecting ideas and teachers, like souvenirs?

Whether the teacher is liked by house pets may not be the most significant question...

What was taught? What are you doing with it?

Ideas must and will stand or fall on their own merits — apart from the character, style, eloquence or breeding of the people who gave them voice.

It's not about *the* teacher or any teacher, but about what you — the student, can do with the teachings...

Robert Thomas
Philosopher...

"A philosopher is someone who practices philosophy, which involves rational inquiry into areas that are outside either theology or science. The term 'philosopher' comes from the Ancient Greek meaning 'lover of wisdom.'"
Wikipedia

The Fifties: Alan Watts & Zen. The Beached Sausalito Ferry Boat. The Beats. Abstract Art. Corbusier and Mies. As both witness and participant, RT was there during the turbulent emergence of what was to become a worldwide wrinkle in the staid fabric of the wisdom tradition called The Human Potential Movement.

Born in 1932 in Middletown, N.Y., he found himself drawn closer to the big city as a student of Art at State University of New York and later of Philosophy at Columbia. As a Commercial Art Director in Manhattan he found himself caught up in the moment, attending classes at the Art Students League and joining friends to attend lectures by Krishnamurti and other visiting luminaries. His early influences; Vedanta, Jung and The Red Book, Judo (Kodokan brown belt), Reich and Whitehead.

That's the Prologue.

Thomas and a friend joined forces to create a Manhattan communications consultancy, and got to work at building a successful business. It was heady! They landed a substantial client list in the first few years while spawning a host of knock-offs. Business was a challenge, but the joy of the sea also called him to a regular sojourn in the cockpit of not one, but many sailing yachts, an Atlantic crossing, and in time, a "Commodore" designation in the Seven Seas Cruising Association. But all that was the day job. Though he hadn't named it, the nucleus of a philosophical platform which resolved the apparent differences between classical philosophy, the "cognitive clearing discipline" and the emergent horizons of particle physics and human potential was steadily taking shape.

It was researched, tested and matured through a long-term series of counseling relationships and eventually, was named Holosophy. Though his life was filled with a series of adventures: blue water sailing, a home in a Spanish villa, a love for special cars and special women; his primary joy was this maturing philosophy. With a young sidekick, he dedicated the remainder of his life to describing his discoveries and developing a body of work which is still expanding.

Unusually for a man of such prodigious gifts, Mr. Thomas did not seek to occupy center stage. He has lived out his years in a quiet beach apartment in Florida, still working, still counseling, still pushing the boundaries of philosophy and researching the farther shores of consciousness and the human condition.

Holosophy. A life work. And a gift.

Return to Foley's Hill
(Summary)

We all have our Foley's Hill experience(s). Life is tough, and hands out all manner of setbacks, failures and tragedy. Many people file those experiences away together into an impenetrable mass of Sub-Rational accumulations: "dark content," connected through a "logical" but not-really-rational web of threatening similarities; waiting to spring into action to "protect us" when triggered by immediate events.

In such moments, we retreat from the present in favor of our remembrances of threatening events long gone, but not forgotten. This is a formula for a life of ever-smaller risks and consequently diminishing rewards — Success Reluctance.

But winning at Life demands that we emerge from our fenced-in zones of safety; to face, embrace and conquer our fear of success. Holosophy was founded to serve this great end.

Every Case is a Character Study. As we build our Character, each of us also creates a unique "Defense Against the New" reflecting our own style and reasoning. We tend to "treasure our cases," even as they cause us to perceive things in ways which limit our freedom of choice.

In "Praxis" we commit to acquiring the skills required to discover that our own mistaken certainties are the very things which set us back. We consistently examine and discard perceptions, practices and psychological constructs which no longer serve a useful purpose. Life leaves marks, but we need not cherish them! Dismantling the chrysalis does not harm, but releases the Being!

"Then, What?" It's time to elevate and expand our views of Ethics and Truth. As we build a larger context, we can see the distant outlines of a more optimal, lofty way of life.

Labyrinthian contemporary culture presents enough noise, confusion and disinformation to shake anyone's confidence. "Commentary" provides balancing advice to aspiring Holosophers.

There. Now it's your turn!

Take this wisdom forward. Improve it where you can. Try not to turn it into a religion.

Through your stable presence, counsel and service, kindle a light and transform the darkness!

Start at the Center

"I think; therefore, I am the center of the universe."
—Craig Bruce

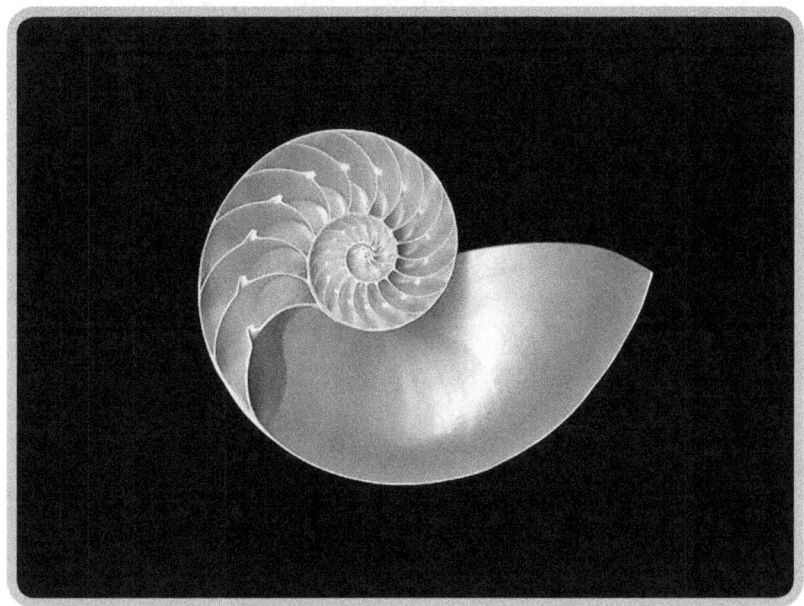

Some parting thoughts...

Begin with your own self-development. Be jealous of your time, and devote yourself to learning everything you can. Vaporize your case, Domain by Domain... Then be a resource to everyone you touch.

Understand that the usual earthly premium on self-development is not so great as on financial acquisition, or cosmetic improvements... Most people are in no particular rush to emerge as fully competent, immortal, luminous beings, nor do they believe that such emergence is even possible. But they will gravitate to your glow and to the honest integrity of your example.

So, glow!

Recognize that there is a hierarchy to development, a naturally expanding order. First, the individual. Then the family. Community. Humanity. Living Things. Cosmos. Aesthetics and the Spirit. Infinity. A Kosmic Rainbow of Domains.

They don't have to be developed in that particular order, but that natural progression gives you a stately incline of accomplishment to which you might choose to dedicate a lifetime.

You are the precise center of a universe. And the precise harmonic at which you choose to resonate is exactly up to you. Try starting with the heart.

J. R. (Jennifer) StJohn
(1952 - 2018)

35 years, 43 countries, with clients in five industries, Ms. StJohn acted as Counselor, Friend, Consultant, and Teacher to individuals and corporations. Demonstrating a plain-spoken directness, hinting at brilliance, tempered by compassion; she was an ally to many. Good things happened when she was around.

A native of the West coast, she migrated to New York in 1980 and fell in love with Manhattan. There, she started her consulting career, dedicated to the proposition that a Fusion of Body, Mind and Spirit are an unbeatable combination for both business and personal relationships.

She was married and divided her time between Florida and Oregon.